THE *Great* ROCKY MOUNTAIN Nature FACTBOOK

A Guide to the Region's Remarkable Animals, Plants, & Natural Features

Susan Ewing

WESTWINDS PRESS™

William Eaton

Go outside and play.

Text © 1999 by Susan Ewing

Library of Congress Cataloging-in-Publication Data:

Ewing, Susan, 1954–
    The great Rocky Mountain nature factbook / by Susan Ewing.
        p.   cm.
    Includes bibliographical references (p.   ) and index.
    ISBN 0-88240-515-2
    1. Natural history—Rocky Mountains.   I. Title.
QH104.5.R6E95   1999
508.78—dc21

                                        98–41240
                                        CIP

WestWinds Press™
An imprint of Graphic Arts Center Publishing Company
P.O. Box 10306, Portland, Oregon 97296-0306, 503-226-2402

President/Publisher: Charles M. Hopkins
Editorial Staff: Douglas A. Pfeiffer, Ellen Harkins Wheat, Timothy W. Frew, Diana S. Eilers, Jean Andrews, Alicia I. Paulson, Deborah J. Loop, Joanna M. Goebel
Production Staff: Richard L. Owsiany, Susan Dupere
Designer: Constance Bollen, cb graphics
Illustrator: Marjorie C. Leggitt, Leggitt Design
Illustration p.177 from photo by Betsy Armstrong
Map art pp.197 and 209: Marjorie Leggitt
Map design: Gray Mouse Graphics

Printed on acid-free recycled paper in the United States of America

CONTENTS

ACKNOWLEDGMENTS

Writers may work by themselves, but it's impossible to write a book like this alone. My special thanks to Susan J. Tweit, whose suggestions, corrections, and remarks revealed not only her understanding of the region but her love for it. Also grateful thanks to Deborah Loop for her supportive facilitation of the project, to editor Linda Gunnarson for her patience and unflagging attention to detail, and to Ellen Wheat for her continuing confidence in my work. And since a picture is worth a thousand words, a million thanks to Marjorie Leggitt for the lively illustrations, and to Constance Bollen for the snappy new design.

Also, for their helpful reviews or checks of material, many thanks to Carl Birkeland, Diane Chalfant, Jeff Connor, Cliff Davis, Rich Fedorchak, Louise Forrest, Steve Gniadek, Kathy Hansen, Roy Kiser, Eric Lane, Will Lanier, Judy McCarthy, Ken Sinay, T.H. Watkins, and Shelly Whitman. Any lingering errors or omissions are, of course, my own.

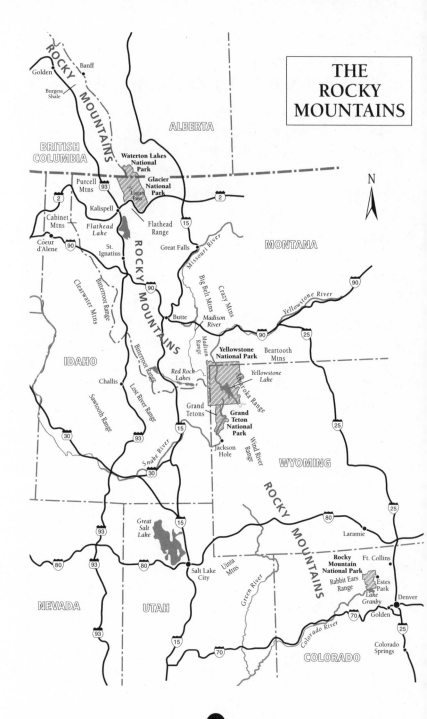

THE ROCKY MOUNTAINS

THE ROCKY MOUNTAINS

An immense, 10,000-mile-long assemblage of mountain ranges stretches all the way from Alaska through South America. In Canada and the Lower 48, the eastern set of ranges in this western cordillera is called the Rocky Mountains.

The Great Rocky Mountain Nature Factbook encompasses a portion of the northern and central Rockies from southern British Columbia to northern Colorado. Hundreds of distinct mountains and ranges mark the territory—their names roll off the tongue and into the imagination: the Front Range, looming over the plains like a stony wave; the Bitterroot, Tobacco Root, Sawtooth, Wind River, Lost River, Salt River, Swan, Goat, Salish, Gros Ventre, Flathead, Absaroka, Mission, Ruby, Pioneer, Lewis, Madison, and Jefferson Ranges. The Beartooth, Beaverhead, Big Belt, Bighorn, Medicine Bow, Salmon River, and Clearwater Mountains. The Crazies.

But of course the Rockies are more than just mountains; in between those uplifted spines of continental crust are lush river valleys, rolling grasslands, and dry, sagebrush flats. This book spotlights a sampling of the plants and animals that live on and between peak and plain, and explores the land that holds them. *The Great Rocky Mountain Nature Factbook* isn't meant to be a field guide. Think of it as an appendix to your field guides on mammals, birds, wildflowers, trees, rocks and minerals, and weather. It's not meant to help you identify the things you see as much as it's meant to help you make sense of what you identify. Use it to satisfy your curiosities about such things as those fat moths that invade your house in seasonal waves (see "Army Cutworm Moth") or how the Rockies formed (see "Mountain Building"). The more you understand, the more you'll want to know. The more you know, the more at home you'll feel. *The Great Rocky Mountain Nature Factbook* is sort of a welcome wagon, then, designed to help you make connections with the community.

The book is arranged into 3 sections for your browsing pleasure: "Animals," "Plants," and "Natural Features," which are identified by thumb tabs on the edge of the pages. Within these sections are smaller groupings, such as "Birds" and "Flowers." The entries themselves are in alphabetical order within each grouping. Initials at the end of each entry in the sections on plants and animals indicate whether you might see that particular species in Glacier National Park (**G**), Yellowstone National Park (**Y**), Grand Teton National Park (**T**), or Rocky Mountain National Park (**R**). Sidebars round out many entries with supplemental overviews, biological esoterica, safety advice, and even a recipe or two.

Finally, a complete index will also help you locate topics of interest within the book, and a list of recommended reading will point you to resources that can further expand your vision of the West.

Travel in the Rockies requires thought and preparation, even in the summer. It can snow in July, and severe winter storms can create wilderness-type hazards, even on road systems. Although summer snow is infrequent, thunderstorms with lightning are routine from late spring into fall.

Elevations higher than those to which people are accustomed can cause dehydration, dizziness, and rapid heartbeat. As reported in the sidebar on acute mountain sickness (in the "Clouds" entry), at 7,000 feet and above our bodies have a harder time absorbing oxygen into the bloodstream. This doesn't just apply to mountain climbers: the nation's highest, paved, through highway is Trail Ridge Road in Rocky Mountain National Park. Open only in the summer, the road runs above 12,000 feet for 4 miles, and above 11,000 feet for 11 miles. At high elevations, drink plenty of water and don't push yourself. Ultraviolet radiation is also more intense, so don't forget sunglasses and sunscreen.

~

I didn't grow up in the Rockies, but I've been growing since I arrived in 1992—finding my own niche on the east side of the Continental Divide among aspen and arrowleaf balsamroot, watching red squirrels and ruffed grouse come and go. Living here has taught me things about my place in the world—the natural world and human society—that I hadn't learned in Alaska or the Pacific Northwest, my homes since early adulthood. It hasn't all been comfortable, especially the human society part. I've had to come to terms with my own presence here, in the face of diminishing wildlife habitats and human pressures on wildlands.

It will take a long time for people to overrun Alaska, and it can be argued that the Pacific Northwest is already a thoroughly occupied land, though with remaining pockets of wilderness. The northern and central Rockies, however, strike me as being somewhere in between, and in the throes of a painful transition. People like me are tipping the balance. I want to live in a quiet, private place, where deer wander by. Yet when 5 more families with the same desires build 5 more houses, the deer vanish.

For a long time, plants, animals, and people in the Rocky Mountain region lived in balance. But with our voracious appetite for space and resources, humans have swept into the West like a full-moon tide and are washing up the sides of the once-remote mountains.

The Rockies sailed into the latter part of the 20th century like an ark upon the plains. Species long extirpated from elsewhere around the continent still live on here, but the ark is leaking. Pressure from urban and suburban development, mining, logging, grazing, and tourism are stressing habitats and wildlife. As you skim through books like this one, learning more about bears, ponderosa pine, and trout, also make an effort to study issues facing the Rocky Mountain West. Tough decisions about natural resources, endangered species, multiple use of public lands, and other volatile issues lie ahead, and the more we know—the more we understand—the better prepared we will be to serve the balance of the community.

· O N E ·

A N I M A L S

ANIMALS

The Rocky Mountains are alive with a rich diversity of wildlife, from bighorn sheep and bears to salamanders and snow fleas. This variety of species springs in large part from the region's wide spectrum of habitats. Because a mountain range has complex topography—including slopes of varying elevation and aspect, canyons, ridges, river valleys, high saddles, and low-lying plains—the amount of sunlight and moisture falling on any given spot is widely variable. A patchwork is created, where moist forests may be situated near dry slopes, which may give way to wet marshes in sight of woodlands, possibly adjacent to grasslands. Animals that rely on specific habitats, such as the wetland-dependent spotted frog, are supported, and generalists such as coyotes and ravens can rove through the mix finding food and shelter year-round.

The following pages present a patchwork of sorts too: a selection of some of the higher-profile and more representative animals of the northern and central Rockies. It's certainly not a complete list, but I hope you will find in it a sense of the region's glorious wholeness— truly one of the greatest beauties of the Rockies. The rugged nature of the terrain, and the fact that humans were slow to populate the isolated, mountainous West, created a de facto wildlife sanctuary where many animals—including the last 60 trumpeter swans in the Lower 48—found refuge. Even today, species long gone from the

East and Midwest, including grizzly bears and mountain lions, still
help spin the ecological web here.

As the Rocky Mountain region becomes more developed, we have a
responsibility to balance our own desires for space and resources with
the needs of wildlife. Our requirements aren't that different: like trout
and dippers, we need clean water; like elk and bison, we rely on
productive soil. And nearly all species are motivated to find safe,
sheltered places to den or raise their young. If we are to preserve the
irreplaceable wholeness of this special place, we have to be willing to
compromise; we are all in this together.

BLUE GROUSE

You're walking through foothill or mountain forests on a lovely spring day and think you hear someone blowing notes on a champagne bottle. What sounds like a stranded reveler is, in reality, a blue grouse. And that deep, resonant *whoot, whoot, whoot, whoot* is the *Dendragapus obscurus* call to amour.

About the size of a small chicken, the male blue grouse is dusky brown with a blackish tail. Male blue grouse often have a pale band at the end of their tail, but for some reason blue grouse of the northern Rockies are missing this marking. Females are a mottled brown.

Male blue grouse also have combs over their eyes that they can raise like Groucho Marx eyebrows.

Courtship is in full swing by early to mid-May. Territorial males can reportedly recognize one another by their distinctive hooting, and, presumably, so can females. Courting males also fan their tails like a turkey and flare certain neck feathers to expose 2 raspberry-colored sacs that inflate to amplify the hoots. When the brown, outer neck feathers are flared, a ring of fine white feathers framing the sac are exposed. Males also have combs over their eyes that they can raise like Groucho Marx eyebrows. For maximum effect, the combs rapidly change color from bright yellow to deep orange-red. To top

• BORN TO RUN •

All chicks are not born equal. Some, such as the offspring of blue grouse, are precocial, born downy and with their eyes open, able to follow their parent within a couple of days. Most game birds, shorebirds, and waterfowl are born precocious. Some precocial young, including grouse, must be shown food, while ducklings, goslings, and cygnets can find their own food as they follow their parent.

Other chicks are altricial at hatching, born naked and with their eyes closed, totally dependent on their parents for nourishment and protection. All passerines (songbirds, or perching birds) are altricial.

According to *The Birder's Handbook*, the female who lays eggs of precocial chicks needs plenty of food while her eggs are forming, to support greater in-egg development. On the other hand, food demands on parents of altricial young are heaviest after the chicks hatch, when they must feed the helpless brood.

As one would suspect, precocial chicks have larger brains at hatching. However, the brains of altricial chicks develop to a greater degree over time, under the care and feeding of their parents. As a result, birds born altricially— including parrots and ravens—generally have larger brains than such precocial birds as grouse and turkeys.

it all off, males advertise their presence with a fluttering jump and wing clap, often eliciting answering claps from other males within hearing distance.

Males and females mate more or less indiscriminately. Females scrape out a shallow depression in which to nest, often hidden under a shrub or the branches of a fallen

tree, and raise young on their own. Not that there's much to it— chicks are born precocial, meaning newborns are downy and mobile, unlike robin chicks, for example, which are born naked and helpless. Grouse chicks are self-sufficient in less than 2 weeks.

As winter comes on, blue grouse actually move higher into

the mountains, usually settling into Douglas-fir forests a few hundred feet below timberline. Blues would rather walk than fly, and they keep walking as snow piles up. In fact, in the winter, blue grouse grow a fringe of flat scales along each toe, turning the foot into a snowshoe. **G, Y, T, R**

BLUEBIRD

Just when it seems winter will last forever, the bluebirds arrive. Snow may still be on the ground when mountain bluebirds return to the Rocky Mountains from southern wintering grounds. Look for the bright blue *Sialia currucoides,* about the size of a very large sparrow, feeding on insects and berries in open areas above 4,000 feet. Males locate good nesting cavities in coniferous trees, aspens, or bluebird boxes, and advertise for prospective mates by calling and fluttering in and out of the hole. Parents take turns feeding chicks on beetles, grasshoppers, and other insects, fetching as many

Bluebird

as 3,000 to 4,000 meals in the 3-week period between hatching and fledging (flying).

Bluebird enthusiasts have found that the best way to entice a nesting pair is to put up a "bluebird trail" of 4 or 5 nest boxes, 100 yards apart. You'll see the wooden boxes on fence posts throughout the West. Mountain, western, and eastern bluebird populations have all declined drastically in this century, probably due to a combination of environmental chemicals, the

• INVASION OF THE CAVITY SNATCHERS •

Around 1890, some 60 European starlings were released into New York City's Central Park by a group wanting to introduce to America all the birds mentioned in Shakespeare's plays. One hundred years later, those 60 have become 200 million, spread from New York to the Pacific Coast. The aggressive *Sturnus vulgaris* has become a serious threat to native cavity nesters in the Rocky Mountain region and elsewhere in the United States, usurping nest holes from bluebirds, flickers, flycatchers, and other species.

The hardy, adaptable birds have associated themselves with humans since the beginning of agriculture and thrive in the wake of converted landscapes. Some control programs have been implemented, but even the destruction of millions of birds seems to put hardly a dent in starling populations.

English sparrows (also called house sparrows, *Passer domesticus*) were introduced from Europe in the mid-19th century because they were attractive and had the potential to control insect pests. The birds, which are really weaver finches and not sparrows, are now a common, abundant—and competitive—species in the United States. These cavity nesters also outcompete bluebirds, swallows, and others for nesting sites and often destroy the eggs and young of less aggressive native species.

Blunders such as these help explain the rigid laws regulating introductions of non-native species.

clearing of standing dead trees, competition for nest sites with exotic species such as starlings and English sparrows, and the switch from wood to metal fence posts. Happily, bluebirds are coming back from this decline; some researchers say populations are recovering in direct proportion to the number of nest boxes installed.

The beautiful, vibrant color of the male bluebird comes not from feather pigment, like the robin's red breast, but from reflected waves of blue light. Blue light waves are reflected out from layers of tiny structures in the bluebird's feathers, similar to the way light reflects off the scales on a butterfly's wing—or off a high, mountain lake.

According to a Pima legend, long ago, bluebirds used to be dull gray. Then one day a flock of the birds found a sparkling lake high in the mountains. They bathed there for 4 days, and when they emerged all their feathers were gone. On the fifth morning, they awoke with brilliant, lake-blue feathers. **G, Y, T, R**

CANADA GOOSE

Few sounds can fill our hearts and raise our eyes like the honkings of migrating Canada geese. The Rocky Mountain chain provides lift and landmarks for the travelers, who seem to capture our attention in a way few other birds do—particularly if the change of season has us feeling restless anyway.

You might see Canada geese—large, grayish brown birds with long black necks, and black heads with white chin straps—in the region at any time of year, but most fly south along the Rockies as far as Mexico for the winter. No one is exactly sure why they fly in the famous V formation. According to one theory, a bird in line gains flight advantage from air currents generated by the bird in front of it. That seems reasonable on paper, but in reality, geese don't maintain the precise, optimum position required to make much difference. Many researchers now believe that geese fly in formation simply because it's a good way to avoid collisions. They apply the same explanation to the honking. Honk if you migrate. Some geese, however, are changing their tune. The proliferation of golf courses, parks, and business complexes with extensive lawns has caused thousands of Canada geese to give up their migratory ways and become permanent, year-round residents. The geese aren't always welcome, as their copious droppings can create both health and aesthetic concerns.

Flocks have a definite hierarchy, and individual family bonds are strong within the flock.

The highest status belongs to family units of parents and offspring, followed by mated pairs without offspring, then singles. The family stays together for a year, enabling young birds to learn from their parents about such things as travel routes, safe rest areas, and how and where to find food. Once back at the breeding grounds, the juveniles set off on their own while the adult pair, who are mated for life, start a new family. The older offspring continue to mature, typically taking a mate in their third year.

Each year before the fall migration, Canada geese molt all their flight feathers simultaneously, rendering the birds flightless for a period of time. This state of vulnerability has undoubtedly contributed to the goose's aggressive nature. Sentinels within the flock keep a constant eye out for danger, even outside the molting season. Canada geese are steadfastly loyal to their mates and families. If a goose gets separated from its mate or offspring, it will launch a frantic, honking search.

Branta canadensis nests on the ground, usually near water. Geese will also use human-constructed platforms—look for large grass-and-stick nests atop platforms installed in lakes or wetlands. Both parents tend the 4 to 7 young, though it's usually the father who leads goslings in the water. If there's a threat, the male puts on a distraction display while the youngsters dive. **G, Y, T, R**

CHICKADEES

Chickadees seem to be everywhere in the Rockies at every season, providing constant, friendly companionship to any outdoor activity.

The black-capped chickadee (*Parus atricapillus*) has a gray back, white belly, black cap and throat, and white cheeks. The mountain chickadee (*P. gambeli*) looks like a slightly sooty version of the black-capped chickadee, with the addition of a white stripe

• FEEDING BACKYARD BIRDS •

During cold months, feeding birds is more than entertaining: it can be an important safety net for winter residents. As natural food sources are used up or buried under snow, a backyard buffet of peanut-butter balls, suet cakes, and sunflower seeds can provide a lifeline for wild birds.

You don't need to know a nuthatch from a nighthawk to begin. All it takes is a well-placed feeder and a little bit of attention. Locate your feeder near cover, but in a spot open enough to expose lurking predators such as house cats. According to the American Bird Conservancy, scientists estimate that free-roaming cats, including pets, strays, and feral cats, kill hundreds of millions of birds in the United States each and every year—from goldfinches and sparrows to endangered plovers.

Supplemental feeding in the summer isn't necessary and can actually be dangerous. Avian diseases are readily spread when birds crowd around feeders, and moldy seed or suet can make birds sick. If you can't commit to keeping your feeder scrupulously clean, don't put it out. Of course, the best alternative is to plant native seed- and fruit-bearing plants around your yard—especially plants that provide food into the winter. Check your local library or bookstore for books about landscaping for wildlife.

over each eye. You'll know both small birds by their cheery *chick-a-dee-dee-dee*.

In summer, chickadees travel in pairs, but they spend the winter gathered in flocks of up to a dozen birds. Typically, 1 or 2 adult pairs will be joined by newly formed pairs of younger birds intending to breed the following spring. The flock may also include a few unattached birds that float between flocks. Mated pairs stay together during the winter, though if a bird dies, a floater may inherit its mate, ensuring that the flock remains stable.

Look and listen for black-capped chickadees in coniferous forests, aspen woods, and stands of willows or cottonwoods.

Mountain chickadees are generally found in higher-elevation coniferous forests, but the 2 chickadees may share a range—and a feeder. Put out some black oil sunflower seeds or suet, and the birds will come looking for you. Feeding chickadees is great winter entertainment and a constant source of inspiration. If these little guys can make it through the season, so can you. Flocks have a definite pecking order; see if you can detect who's who as they come to your feeder, one at a time, to grab and go.

Chickadees aren't totally dependent on your food bank; the busy birds have been stashing thousands of seeds and insects over the course of the summer, not forming central caches, but hiding single food items all over the place.

Researchers have found that chickadees have a specific enzyme that enables them to deposit fat quickly. This fat is stored during the day and used up overnight.

During cold weather, chickadees roost together in tree cavities for warmth and security. The colder and windier the night, the tighter they cram in. Look for bent tail feathers the next morning. Chickadees also tolerate the cold by going into mini-hibernation each night, allowing their body temperature to drop from about 110°F to as low as 50°F. This daily dormancy reduces heat loss and energy demand by minimizing the difference between body and air temperatures. In the morning, shivering serves to bring the birds' body temperatures back up. **G, Y, T, R**

CLARK'S NUTCRACKER

There is such elegance in the design of a mountain ecosystem. Take, for instance, the relationship between Clark's nutcracker and the whitebark pine, a tree of high-elevation rocky slopes. Plenty of animals in the Rockies collect and eat whitebark pine nuts, but only the nutcracker gathers and stores the nuts at a depth at which they'll sprout, in habitat capable of supporting new trees. Nutcracker and pine are thought to have coevolved. The bird's bill became longer over the years, perfecting it for prying pine seeds from cones. A special expandable pouch developed under its tongue, enabling it to carry more seeds. The tree seems to have evolved cones and seeds that grow and ripen in a cycle that maximizes their chance of being collected and buried (essentially planted) by the nutcracker. This isn't just a design flourish; researchers have shown that Clark's nutcracker is an essential component of whitebark pine reproduction.

You will almost certainly see or hear *Nucifraga columbiana* on trips into forested mountains in both summer and winter. The nutcracker is about the size and shape of a small crow, with a light gray body and head, black tail, and black wings with white

Clark's Nutcracker

patches. Listen for its harsh *khraa, khraa, khraa* coming from the tops of evergreens. This bird can get as tame as its similar-looking camp robber (gray jay) cousin.

The pine nut caches are an important winter food source and also provide a ready resource in spring, when parents are raising chicks. Because of this security, nutcrackers can nest early, when snow is still deep. Both parents sit on eggs and brood young.

Nutcrackers can carry more than 3 dozen nuts at a time in their pouches. Over the summer and early fall, one bird might stash up to 33,000 pine nuts, with only 4 to 5 nuts per cache. Many seeds are buried on windswept or south-facing slopes that don't accumulate much snow, leaving the seeds more available throughout the winter. Experiments have shown that nutcrackers don't just forage for hidden seeds, but actually remember where their piles are hidden. The birds use landmarks such as rocks, can estimate distance, and can recall directions over a period of many months.

An individual bird may retrieve only 1,000 stashed seeds per year, leaving about 97 percent of the seeds in the ground. Other birds and animals raid the caches, but there are still plenty of seeds left to sprout. If you see 3 or 4 seedlings growing close together on a windy slope, you can guess they are the products of nutcracker plantings. **G, Y, T, R** (See Gray Jay; Limber Pine)

DIPPER

Found solely in mountainous regions of western North America, the slate-gray dipper is something of a good-luck bird in the Rockies. You'll feel charmed to see it standing on a rock alongside a cold, mountain stream doing its knee bends (dipping), or flying low above the rushing water. You'll be all the more enchanted to see this plump, bluebird-size songbird plunk into the current

Dipper

and disappear, even on a cold, winter day.

There's nothing like having an ecological niche all to yourself. *Cinclus mexicanus* is the only aquatic songbird in the world. Dippers use stubby wings to propel themselves down to the gravelly streambed (sometimes more than 20 feet under water) and then grasp rocks with their strong toes to walk upstream. As they go, they glean insect larvae from rocks and water. Aquatic invertebrates comprise the largest portion of the dipper's diet, but the birds also eat tiny fish and adult insects. Dippers and trout have very similar food requirements, making dippers an indicator of healthy streams.

Obviously, this is not your typical tweety bird. The bird formerly known as water ouzel has an extremely large, oil-rich preening gland, more like that of a swan than a songbird, and the dipper is dry as a duck as soon as it steps out of the water. Under its feather slicker, the dipper has a thick layer of down to keep itself warm even in extremely cold temperatures. Underwater, a movable flap covers each nostril and a special membrane protects the dipper's eyes.

Both sexes have a melodious song, which you may be lucky enough to hear even in winter. As long as a spring or thermal feature keeps the dipper's home stream from freezing, the bird stays put. If the stream ices over, the dipper must move downstream until it finds open water.

Pair bonds aren't long-lasting, but courtship is expressive and sometimes includes the male and female displaying together, jumping up with breasts touching. The female usually builds her nest where spray from a stream will keep it moist, such as on a midstream rock, or among ferns and mosses on a cliff face near or behind a waterfall. Constructed of moss, the nest is shaped like a little domed hut with an arched entrance near the bottom. It's not unusual for a dipper to raise 2 broods in a single season, using the same nest, but often having different mates. **G, Y, T, R**

GOLDEN EAGLE

Golden eagles (*Aguila chrysaetos*) belong to the wide open spaces of the Rocky Mountain West. Unlike their bald eagle cousins, who are always found near water and trees, goldens prefer rockier mountain habitats and rolling, intermountain plains. You might see them in any season, as goldens are year-round residents of the region. They're most visible to the casual observer in spring, when they hang out along highways eating road-killed ground squirrel.

Named for the wash of gold on their neck feathers, adult goldens are a solid brown bird with a wingspan of about 7 feet—nearly the same size as a bald eagle. Adult goldens and balds are easily distinguished by the bald eagle's bright white head and tail, but immature birds are harder to tell apart. Immature bald eagles are mottled brown-and-white, and immature goldens are brown with a bright white rump patch.

• RAPTOR FAMILY TREE •

The term "raptor" comes from the Latin for "plunderer" and refers to birds of prey. There are 2 distinct families of day-hunting raptors: the hawks, or Accipitridae family, and the falcons, or Falconidae family. With a little practice, you can begin to distinguish between families and subgroups by a bird's overall shape and style of flight.

Within the hawk family are eagles, buteos, accipiters, and harriers. Eagles are massive birds with great wingspans and large heads and bills. Both bald and golden eagles have relatively slow wing beats, and the birds soar whenever possible. Bald eagles live near water, eating fish and ducks; golden eagles live in drier country, subsisting on small mammals.

Buteos, such as the red-tailed and rough-legged hawks, are stocky birds with broad wings and wide tails. Their chief foods include rodents and rabbits. Look for them perching on telephone poles or soaring and circling in the open sky.

Accipiters, including the goshawk, sharp-shinned hawk, and Cooper's hawk, have smallish heads, longish tails, and short, rounded wings. They hunt and eat primarily birds, filling in with small mammals. Watch for accipiters flying with rapid wing beats interspersed with glides.

Harriers are slender birds with slim, rounded wings and long tails. The only North American species, the northern harrier, used to be known as the marsh hawk. Look for its low, gliding flight—sometimes just a few feet off the ground—following the contours of the land as it hunts for small rodents.

While the hawk family has many subgroups, a falcon is a falcon. These streamlined birds, which include the kestrel, merlin, peregrine, and prairie falcons, have long, pointed wings and relatively long tails. Falcons rarely soar and are most often seen flying with rapid, shallow-stroke wing beats. Kestrels may be the most visible of the group, as they are relatively common and like to perch on telephone wires. Also watch for kestrels hovering in midair over grassy highway margins as they look for prey.

Owls are also birds of prey, although the term is most commonly used to refer to day-hunting birds.

Goldens will scavenge when the opportunity arises, but prefer to hunt for a living, using their extremely acute vision to detect prey. The eyes of a 10-pound golden eagle are about twice the size of human eyes, allowing a large image to be cast on the retina.

A big eye also accommodates a high number of rods and cones—photoreceptor cells sensitive to light and color. Eagle eyes don't move in their sockets, so the bird must turn its head to look around.

Although the golden eagle has a formidable beak, it catches, and usually kills, prey with its talons. Each of the eagle's 4 toes is equipped with a talon; the hind talon is biggest, at about 2½ inches long. Goldens can purportedly exert 1,400 pounds of pressure per square inch of mammal skull. Their primary prey are ground squirrels and other small rodents in summer and hares in winter. Under certain circumstances, golden eagles will also take antelope fawns, mountain goat kids, and bighorn sheep lambs. Goldens will also occasionally prey on the young of domestic sheep and goats. Their depredation on the livestock industry as a whole is minimal, though eagles can have an impact on individual flocks.

Golden eagles build huge stick nests on cliff faces and occasionally in trees. Lifelong pairs may rebuild the same nest year after year; old nests can be 6 feet across and 5 feet deep. They often build 2 or 3 nests in their territory and alternate using them, presumably to control infestations of lice, ticks, mites, and other pests brought to the nest on prey. Bald eagles build just 1 nest, but of course their primary prey, fish, aren't bothered by fleas.

As with most raptors, the female can be a third larger than the male. This might be insurance against possible aggression toward the young when the male comes to deliver food. The male feeds the female in the nest, but only rarely feeds the young directly. A brood of 2 is most common, though the larger chick sometimes kills the smaller.

Golden eagles have been protected since 1962, after a decade in which more than 20,000 were killed because of

• DABBLERS AND DIVERS •

A place for everything, everything in its place. Nature is nothing if not organized. Take ducks, for instance. Imagine the tension and inefficiency if every duck on a pond was going after the same food. Evolution doesn't seem to favor free-for-alls, so ducks developed into a society of dabblers and divers. Biologists call it "resource partitioning," whereby animals specialize in ways that allow species to coexist without being in direct competition.

Dabblers feed on or near the surface of the water, tipping bottom-up to reach aquatic vegetation or invertebrates in shallow water, or to snatch food suspended near the water's surface in deeper water. They also forage on land for seed and waste grain. Dabblers, such as teal, mallards, and pintails, have large wings relative to their body size and are fairly slow fliers, able to land in tight spots and capable of taking off vertically.

Divers have large feet set on short legs situated far back on the duck's body. This allows them to propel themselves completely underwater to forage for vegetation and invertebrates living at greater depths. These ducks, including canvasbacks, redheads, and scaups, have smaller wings and fly faster than dabblers, but they land and take off more like airplanes than helicopters, so need larger bodies of water.

perceived threats to the livestock industry. Their numbers are now stable and even increasing in some areas. **G, Y, T, R**

GOLDENEYES

It's astonishing to see ducks paddling cheerfully around in an open spot of river on a bitter, winter day—almost enough to make you forget your own cold feet.

About the size of a small mallard, the goldeneye is one of the few ducks that remain in the region year-round. There are 2 species of *Bucephala:* the common goldeneye (*B. clangula*), which ranges widely throughout the West, and Barrow's, or Rocky Mountain, goldeneye (*B. islandica*), whose more limited range happily includes the

Rockies. Look for both species on lakes and large rivers.

The male Barrow's has a black head with a steep forehead and a white, crescent-shaped patch between his bill and his eye— which is indeed golden. His back is black with white barring; chest and belly are white. The common goldeneye has more of a greenish black head, a flatter forehead, and the white face patch is rounder. Females of both species have brownish gray bodies with brown heads and a white collar.

Goldeneyes are diving ducks, able to remain submerged for nearly a minute at a time while foraging on the bottom for aquatic insects, crayfish, and vegetation.

In the spring, watch for courting males kicking sprays of water to the sky. Pair bonds may last over consecutive years, although the male doesn't take part in incubating eggs or rearing the brood. The female selects the nest site—preferably in a tree cavity near the water—and often

returns to the same spot each breeding season. The precocious ducklings leave the nest before they are able to fly and so have developed the ability to tumble down without injuring themselves. Once out of the nest, the ducklings never go back.

As goldeneyes take flight, listen for the wing-whistling sound that gives them their common name, "whistler." **G, Y, T, R**

GRAY JAY

You're relaxing at the edge of a mountain meadow, relishing a snack of cheese and crackers after a long hike, when you get the feeling someone is watching. You get up and scan the quiet scene with your binoculars, and when you go back to your cheese, you discover you've been robbed.

Don't feel bad. Gray jays, or "camp robbers" as they're fondly called, have been known to steal bacon right out of a frying pan. *Perisoreus canadensis* presents an interesting challenge to the rules against feeding wildlife.

You don't have to search for these birds—chances are they'll find *you* when you stop for lunch along a Rocky Mountain trail or at a picnic area or campground near forests of lodgepole pine, spruce, or fir. The gray jay is a fluffy-looking gray bird, a bit larger and stockier than a robin, with a white forehead and whitish underside. (It may be confused with Clark's nutcracker, a slightly larger bird with black wings and a much longer beak.) Like juveniles of many other species, young gray jays sport brown plumage before growing into their adult coloring. Gray jays often travel in family groups, the better to rip you off. These birds have been following people through the woods since there were people to follow; their other name, whiskey jack, comes

> **Gray jays, or "camp robbers" as they're fondly called, have been known to steal bacon right out of a frying pan.**
>
> ●

from a variation on the Indian word *wis-ka-tjon.*

Like other members of the Corvid family (which includes ravens, crows, and magpies), gray jays have an interesting vocal repertoire of various calls and whistles, including pretty good imitations of the red-tailed hawk and northern pygmy owl. John James Audubon noticed that the eastern blue jay used its hawk call imitations to flush songbirds off nests so that the jay could steal eggs and nestlings. Perhaps the gray jay does this as well. When not stealing the voices of other birds, the gray jay's own call is a soft *whee-ah.*

Also like other members of the Corvid family, gray jays like to cache food. In their personal twist on the habit, they use a large salivary gland to secrete sticky mucus and make a bolus of food that can be stashed in tree crevices. Besides cheese and crackers, gray jays collect grasshoppers, bees, wasps, nuts, bird eggs, small nestlings of other species, and carrion when food is short in winter.

Because gray jays often begin nesting early in the spring, their nests are extremely well insulated. Usually located in the crotch of a tree, the nests are bulky, well-woven constructions of sticks, bark strips, moss, and grass, held together with silk from spider webs and cocoons, and lined with feathers, fur, and more bark and grass. **G, Y, T, R** (See Clark's Nutcracker)

HAIRY WOODPECKER

Think of woodpeckers as the forest's Housing Development Authority. Each cavity they excavate for their own use provides future housing for other cavity nesters such as chickadees, house wrens, tree swallows, bluebirds, and sometimes nuthatches. This is important because a lack of nest holes can be more of a limiting factor for some species than a lack of food.

You might run into the relatively common hairy woodpecker nearly anyplace in the Rockies with trees, from evergreen forests and aspen groves to city parks and cemeteries. Listen for high-speed rapping or slower, duller, tap-tapping sounds, or a sharp, vocal *peek!* The hairy is slightly smaller than a robin, with a bright white breast and black wings checkered with white. Its head is black with white streaks above and below the eye. The male has a bright red patch on the back of its head. *Picoides villosus* looks like the larger twin of the downy woodpecker, *P. pubescens,* except the hairy's bill is as long as its own head, and the downy's bill is not.

The hairy is specialized for woodwork. Its sturdy bill is shaped like a chiseled pickax, and the bird can position itself quite securely as it gets down to business. Like most members of

• SNAGS •

Standing dead trees are known as snags, although some naturalists have taken to calling them "wildlife trees." Dead trees still have lots of value to an ecosystem, especially as places to nest. Even when food is abundant, bird and mammal populations can suffer if suitable nesting and denning sites aren't available.

Woodpeckers excavate nesting holes in snags, which in succeeding years may be appropriated by chickadees, nuthatches, and a variety of other cavity nesters. Mammals that den in tree cavities include squirrels, martens, mice, and black bears.

Besides providing homes, snags can be sources of food for birds too, as dead trees are often hosts to beetles and other insects. And birds on the hunt, from hawks to flycatchers, use snags as lookout perches.

New logging practices include leaving some standing trees in the middle of cuts and actually topping live trees to create snags. And there are rumors of a few bird-loving homeowners installing dead trees in their yards in the ultimate attempt to lure a greater variety of avian company.

the Picidae family, the hairy woodpecker has strong feet especially designed for grasping vertical surfaces, with 2 toes pointing forward and 2 pointing back (zygodactyl feet). Super-stiff tail feathers provide bracing support.

Besides making holes, woodpeckers use their bills to pry under bark and into wood for insects. But they don't catch prey in their bills. For that, they have one of the most amazing tongues in the avian world. It's way too long to fit in the bill, so the tongue is retractable, winding up inside the skull. Imagine for a moment that you have a super-long tongue. Now imagine shooting it out at some target and then whipping back the slack from the base so that it loops sort of like a fly line, snaking up inside the back of your skull and curving around until the tip of your tongue comes to rest nicely in your mouth.

The tongue tip is a rigid, barbed lance that the bird uses to spear grubs and other prey at the far end of bore holes. The woodpecker's tongue is also coated with sticky saliva to help hold prey on the retrieve.

Hairy woodpeckers are nonmigratory, staying in the Rockies all year. Pairs form during the winter and probably remain together only for the duration of the breeding season.

The male usually selects the nest site, and both parents participate in incubating eggs and tending young. The female incubates the eggs during the day, while the male commonly takes the night shift. Parents continue to tend their brood of about 4 chicks for several weeks after they've learned to fly. **G, Y, T, R**

HUMMINGBIRD

Although most attention is usually focused on grand-scale features of the Rocky Mountain region—massive peaks, huge elk, statuesque eagles—we have some extraordinary small treasures too. Calliope hummingbirds, for instance. Found only in the West, *Stellula*

Hummingbird

calliope is the smallest bird living in the United States. About the size of your little finger, the calliope winters in Mexico and spends summers in the open forests, mountain meadows, and willow and alder thickets of the Rockies.

The male is brilliant green with a throat patch of flaming, reddish purple feathers that flare like rays when he's agitated. English ornithologist and artist John Gould named this bird after Kalliope, the Greek Muse of heroic poetry. Anyone who maintains a nectar feeder can attest to the calliope's sense of epic heroics—or just plain bravado. Male calliopes will impatiently buzz a human until the feeder is hung and then aggressively defend its territory against encroachment by other males.

Watch for courting behaviors near feeders. Males make a U-shaped display flight, diving as much as 65 feet and then swooping back up. Air rushing through feathers produces a loud *bzt* at the foot of the dive. Males also sweep back and forth like a pendulum while courting.

The female, who looks similar to the male, only without the red throat patch, builds a tiny, well-camouflaged nest of moss and shredded bark, lined with plant down, covered with lichen, and bound with the silk of spider webs and cocoons. She usually lays 2 eggs, which are only slightly larger than Tic Tacs, and tends her young alone, feeding them a liquid food from her crop. Besides nectar, hummingbirds eat insects, spiders, and tree sap.

Hummingbirds can't walk, but they're the only bird that can fly backward. They also fly straight up, straight down, sideways, and can truly hover. In hovering flight, the hummer moves its wings in a sort of figure-8 pattern. As explained in *The Birder's Handbook*, hummingbirds have an extremely mobile shoulder joint, allowing them to twist the wing in a way that generates lift on both

• NEOTROPICAL MIGRANTS, OR ¿SE HABLA TWEET? •

An amazing variety of avian travelers can be found along the Rocky Mountain chain, which serves as a highway for migrating birds. Some travel north as far as the Arctic, while other neotropical migrants (birds that winter in the tropics and migrate north for the summer), such as robins, hummingbirds, and western tanagers, make their summer homes here. Generally speaking, migrant songbirds of the Rockies are thought to winter from central Mexico to the Amazon Basin. Shorebirds might winter from the Mexican border all the way south to Tierra del Fuego.

An abundance of food and nesting opportunities have drawn birds north for countless generations, although it appears as though the western landscape is becoming less supportive of migrating birds. Add to that the destruction of habitat south of the border, and the combined impact is troubling.

Recently, more effort has been put into researching the effects of habitat loss and alteration on neotropical migrants, but there's still a lot we don't know. The United States is estimated to have about two-thirds as many acres of timber as were present when the Pilgrims arrived, but the nature of the woods has been transformed. In areas that have been logged and replanted, a once diverse ecosystem has become a monoculture of uniform canopy and meager understory.

Agriculture may have increased the amount of some foods available, but at the same time croplands reduce the variety of food resources for wild birds and potentially eliminate nesting opportunities. Also, industrial pesticides may entirely exterminate insects, removing a natural food resource that is especially crucial for nestlings. Established suburban neighborhoods often offer a wide selection of mature trees for nesting, but domestic cats, dogs, crows, cars, and other dangers pose unnatural threats to survival.

The cowbird, a native species that has thrived in our altered landscape, lays eggs in the nests of other species. The much larger cowbird hatchling, which usually matures more quickly than its nest mates, may outcompete the others for food and be the only one to survive. The invasion of non-native birds that compete for nest sites, and the spread of noxious weeds that may not favor native species, also threaten neotropical migrants.

the backward and forward wing strokes. The front edge of the wing leads on both strokes, and on the backstroke the underside of the wing faces up. With each wing beat (there are 20 to 80 per second), the bird is able to make use of the lift created by the previous stroke. **G, Y, T, R**

MAGPIE

One of the first questions visitors to the Rockies are likely to ask is, "What's that big, beautiful, black-and-white bird?" It may take old-timers a minute to answer the question, since they might not put "beautiful" and "magpie" in the same sentence. Instead, they're likely to associate the bird with such words as "roadkill" or "garbage dump." But the magpie *is* beautiful, as well as smart, interesting, and even beneficial.

Visitors Lewis and Clark also noticed the bird. They sent President Jefferson four magpies, one of which made it all the way to Washington, via New Orleans and Florida, where it was housed in the visitors' room of the White House.

Members of the Corvid family, along with ravens, crows, and jays, magpies are about the size of crows and sport a jet-black hood and back, snow-white belly and shoulders, and a long, sweeping, black tail. In sunlight, the black feathers shine with blue iridescence. Look for magpies in just about any Rocky Mountain habitat under 8,000 feet or so, at any time of year. The gregarious birds are common along roadsides, cleaning up the remains of small and large mammals killed by motorists.

Magpies don't rely solely on speeding vehicles or garbage dumps to make a living. These clever corvids are adept at catching grasshoppers, cutworms, and other agricultural pests, as well as mice and snakes. They will also rob songbird eggs and chicks from nests—a habit that contributes to their villainous reputation. If you're really lucky, you'll spy a magpie pacing back and forth from head to hind end on a patient deer, bighorn sheep, or other large mammal, rummaging around in its hide for ticks or other insects to eat. The hoofed hosts seem generally agreeable to magpies searching around their ears and tails.

Like ravens and crows, magpies work together in shenanigans designed to steal food from predators. For instance, a team of magpies will land at a carcass controlled by a coyote or golden eagle and commence patrolling the perimeter, just out of reach. Eventually, one of the magpies will find an opportunity to peck the predator's rump or pull its tail. When the mark wheels to snap at the intruder, another gang member dashes in to snatch whatever it can carry off.

Magpies form long-term pair bonds. Male and female work together to create a large, messy dome of sticks with

Magpie on Bighorn Sheep

two entrances in which to raise young. In the center, a mud bowl nest is lined with hair and fine roots and stems. The female lays about 7 eggs, taking care of incubation duties while the male feeds her. Both parents feed the young. If a magpie loses its mate early in the breeding season, a noisy flock of callers gathers within 24 hours. Perhaps this is why a flock of magpies is known as a "tidings."

Magpies have a rather harsh *rak rak rak* call, but are capable of learning words in captivity. **G, Y, T, R**

MEADOWLARK

Turn off the car air conditioner and open the window. You wouldn't want to miss the music of the meadowlarks. The western meadowlark is the state bird of Montana and Wyoming, as well as North Dakota, Nebraska, Kansas, and Oregon. It's not necessarily thought of as a mountain bird, but the meadowlark does inhabit the high-elevation grasslands that are as much a part of the Rocky Mountain ecosystem as alpine peaks. Look and listen for them in grasslands, cultivated fields, pastures, meadows, and intermountain prairies.

About the size of a small robin, *Sturnella neglecta* is a light, variegated brown above with a bright yellow breast. A distinctive black V crosses the chest like a loose scarf. Some Rocky Mountain meadowlarks stay put for the winter; others migrate south as far as central Mexico.

This bird of open spaces nests on the ground, constructing a sort of grass tent with a hole in the side. If available, horsehair is often incorporated into the construction. The female incubates eggs, which hatch in about 2 weeks. The male helps feed the average 5 young, which are able to fly in about 12 days. Meadowlarks eat primarily insects, supplemented by seeds.

Sturnella's well-loved, gurgling song is a variable, 7- to 10-note pattern of reedy tones. Listen for double notes in some songs. Males have a repertoire of 5 to 12 song types. Females recognize males more by their call notes than by their songs, so the songs are probably used to communicate territoriality to other males. Eastern meadowlarks have a simpler vocalization composed of 2 slurred notes.

According to the auditory template hypothesis, each bird species is born with a neurological model of what its song should sound like. Individual birds presumably develop their songs by matching the sounds they hear with the song templates in their brains. Meadowlarks are thought to imprint songs during the first few months of life. **G, Y, R**

RAVEN

Long ago, Raven the Trickster stole the moon and hung it in the sky. The moon still shines, and Raven still walks among us, looking for shiny treasures.

Ravens are nearly everywhere in the Rockies, adapted to nearly every habitat type the region has to offer. The tough, resourceful birds stick around all year, hunting with the hunters, skiing with the skiers, trailing the hikers, and hanging out at restaurant dumpsters in the slack times.

Black as a moonless night, ravens are about 2 feet long from heavy beak to spade-shaped tail. This makes them the largest passerine, or perching bird, and the largest all-black bird in the world. They have a wide repertoire of vocalizations, from a simple *tok* to various melodic croaks. *Corvus corax* is adept at imitating sounds and may reserve one it has learned to use as a unique call. An agitated bird may cry for its mate by mimicking that special call and, if it is within earshot, the mate will come immediately.

In winter, ravens may gather in flocks, but pairs break off on their own as spring approaches.

• TILL DEATH DO US PART, OR NOT •

Birds take 1 of 4 basic approaches to breeding: monogamy, polygyny, promiscuity, and polyandry. Monogamy is far and away the most typical arrangement. Up to 90 percent of bird species are monogamous; this includes pairs that stay together through a single breeding cycle (such as house wrens), birds that remain paired for a few seasons (robins and tree swallows), and birds that have the same mate their entire lives (eagles, swans, and ravens).

Obviously, monogamy must have its advantages. After a pair is established, courting energy can be channeled into producing eggs and nourishing and protecting offspring. Even without the presence of young, a pair of adult birds can cooperate in finding food and protecting each other.

The disadvantage to monogamy is that all a bird's eggs are in one basket, so to speak. The reproductive investment is higher, so loss of a brood or mate is more costly.

However, recent DNA testing has shown that even monogamous pairs may have outside dalliances. Biologically, this makes sense, as genetic diversity is enhanced, and males and females can hedge against an infertile mate or unsuccessful brood.

Polygyny is the next most common strategy, in which a male is attentive to an average of 2 females. Western meadowlarks practice polygyny. In cases where the female has her choice of males, she will choose the strongest, most aggressive individual since he is most likely to control a territory with the best food and nesting resources. This is important because most polygynous males don't help females raise young.

Promiscuity, in which males and females breed indiscriminately with no bonding, is relatively uncommon among birds. In this case, male and female get together only to mate, after which the female goes off to build a nest and raise her young. Hummingbirds and grouse are promiscuous.

Less than 1 percent of bird species practice polyandry, in which a female breeds with more than 1 male. Polyandry is found mostly among shorebirds, including phalaropes and mountain plovers. Interestingly, the males in polyandrous relationships may perform all or most of the parenting tasks, and females are often larger and more colorful. Those unexpected attributes led John James Audubon to misidentify the sexes in his phalarope prints.

Unpaired juveniles often band together in raucous gangs. Ravens, which may live more than 20 years, form long-term pair bonds. Near nesting time mates stay close, walking and flying together or perching on fences, two by two. The male may offer

Ravens

his head to the female to preen, and the two touch bills frequently. Preferred nest sites are on cliffs or, if necessary, in evergreen trees. Male and female work together to build or repair their nest, and the male feeds the female while she's incubating 4 to 6 eggs. Raven families often stay together through the first winter.

Ravens are accomplished fliers and appear to relish practicing their aerobatics. The half-roll must be as fun to perform as it is to watch: look for a raven to tuck its wing in midair, roll onto its back, and roll up again. You might also see birds tumbling together through the air, or flying wing tip to wing tip.

Ravens are about as opportunistic as birds come, feeding on carrion, bird eggs and nestlings, insects, seeds, fruit, garbage, dog food, and whatever. Although they have a scavenger's reputation, ravens are clever predators, catching mice and other small vertebrates, sometimes by using teamwork.

Birds in the Corvid family, which includes ravens, crows, jays, and magpies, are believed to be on an avian intelligence par with mynas and parrots. In some experiments, ravens performed abstract tasks as well as chimpanzees. In his fascinating book *Ravens in Winter,* Bernd Heinrich quotes behavioral ecologist

W. A. Montevecchi as saying that, compared to ravens, seagulls act like "vegetables." **G, Y, T, R**

ROSY FINCH

The best thing about a spell of particularly harsh weather is that it can drive throngs of rosy finches to backyard bird feeders. A flock of the stocky finches can put one in mind of a crowd of avian dignitaries, formally attired in gray-black plumage with dusky raspberry wings, black forehead, and soft-gray crown.

In a way, *Leucosticte arctoa* are ambassadors of Rocky Mountain snowfields. In early summer, rosy finches flock at the receding snow line (*Leucosticte* means "white line"), searching for insects and seeds. When bugs land on snow, they become sluggish with the cold, making them easier prey, and rosy finches take advantage of this.

The active birds, slightly larger than house finches, spend a lot of time on the ground walking, rather than hopping, as they forage.

Rosy finches nest and summer in the high country, often well above timberline in grassy or rocky areas. Males of this species seem to outnumber females 6 to 1, so the breeding season is lively, with lots of fighting. The female chooses a nest site and constructs her own nest, to which she may return year after year. Built among rock piles or on cliffs, nests are bulky affairs of moss, grasses, lichens, rootlets, and leaves, lined with fine grass, hair, and ptarmigan feathers. The male feeds the incubating female, and both parents feed the 4 to 5 chicks, packing food for nestlings into special pouches that open through the floor of the mouth. Clark's nutcrackers—corvid relatives of magpies and ravens—often destroy rosy finch nests, eggs, and young.

When the weather turns cold, rosy finches move to lower elevations where snow is less deep. They sometimes gather in huge numbers, roosting in mine shafts or caves in flocks of over

• THE OTHER MIGRATION •

The word "migration" typically conjures images of animals such as bison, gray whales, and Arctic terns covering hundreds if not thousands of miles on long-distance peregrinations. But there's another kind of seasonal migration in which an animal's travel involves feet of elevation rather than miles of distance. Altitudinal migration occurs when animals move to a lower elevation in the face of winter's cold and snow.

Deer and elk are among the hoofed animals that move to lower-elevation winter ranges when snow piles up. When the animals head back to higher country in the summer, winter range has time to recover so that it can sustain wildlife populations through the next snow season.

Rosy finches and mountain chickadees are among the bird species that move down a zone or two in the winter as food gets harder and harder to find at higher elevations. (See Home on the Winter Range)

1,000 birds. Rosy finches spend the winter in the abandoned nests of cliff swallows. **G, Y, T, R**

SANDHILL CRANE

Their high hosannas fill the sky—a reedy, rolling, cackling cacophony that seems part of the very atmosphere itself. You'll probably hear sandhill cranes before you see them. Their voices can be ventriloquial, sometimes making it hard to tell if cranes are overhead, over here, or over there. The long-legged, 3½-foot-tall cranes pack in extra sonority by having a 5-foot-long windpipe voice box that coils like a French horn.

The pewter-gray bird has a bright red crown and long, spearlike bill. Cranes don't winter in the Rockies, but thousands make their summer homes in the prairies, marshes, and sloughs of the region. The huge, migrating flocks disperse when they arrive, so during the summer you're most likely to see or hear cranes either in pairs or in smaller flocks.

Keep an eye open in wet meadows, in farm fields, and near rivers. What you really want to see are cranes dancing. They dance at all times of year for a variety of reasons (such as expressing agitation, dominance, or submission), but the most elaborate cotillion seems to accompany the spring mating season. Vertical leaps form the core of crane choreography. From a crouch, the cranes explode as high as 15 feet into the air, heads tilted to the heavens, spreading their 6- to 7-foot wingspans, legs dangling. They bow and curtsy. In seeming exuberance, they toss sticks or clumps of grass into the air and stab at them as they come down. In a flock, one dancing bird may inspire the entire group to join in.

Even long-mated pairs dance as a way to reconfirm their bond. *Grus canadensis* mates for life, apparently "dating" several prospective partners over a 3- to 4-year period before finally taking a permanent mate. Sandhill cranes can live to be more than 20 years old, so pairs may have years of valuable experience in surviving and raising young together.

Both male and female are attentive parents. Together, they build a nest of grasses or reeds on the ground in a wet meadow, on a vegetated sandbar, or near a riverbank. The female lays an average of 2 eggs, though it's not unusual for the larger chick to kill the smaller before leaving the nest. This siblicide has been recorded even in times of plenty. Precocious young cranes can walk almost immediately upon hatching and are soon catching their own insects, even though parents feed their young for up to 6 months and guide their behavior until the next breeding cycle.

Sandhill cranes are among the most omnivorous of birds, feeding on insects, seeds, grains, berries, worms, eggs, grass, roots, lichens,

Sandhill Cranes

frogs, mice, and aquatic plants. Look for them feeding on waste grain in stubble fields. Cranes feel safest roosting with their feet in the water, so also watch for them in the evening flying toward a river or wetland.

In late summer and early fall, cranes begin to "stage," or gather into large flocks, for their southward migration. After a number of days, on some unseen cue, the big birds circle together to the top of a thermal to glide off toward their winter homes. The Teton Basin of Idaho and San Luis Valley of Colorado are among the region's major staging areas.

G, Y, T, R

SNIPE

Yes, there is such a thing as a snipe, and shorebirds do live in the Rocky Mountains. This cousin to the eastern woodcock lives in wet farm pastures, wetlands, muskegs, and along sloughs throughout most of the region. Some snipe winter in the Rocky Mountain states, but most head south, spreading themselves from California to Brazil.

Your best chances of seeing *Gallinago gallinago* are to almost step on it. The mottled brown bird relies on its cryptic coloring for camouflage, responding to danger by sitting tight. At the last possible second, the snipe will burst out of its hiding place and fly zigzagging away, crying sharp notes of alarm.

A snipe looks something like a large sandpiper. It stands about 8 inches tall on long, skinny legs and has a thin, distinctive bill about 2½ inches long. The bird's name derives from the Anglo-Saxon word for "snout." The hard but flexible bill is sensitive on the end, allowing the snipe to detect what's in the mud as it probes for food. Although snipe are capable of catching crickets and other insects on the fly, most of their

food is obtained in the first ½-inch of soil. Snipe eat insect larvae, worms, beetles, spiders, mollusks, and crustaceans. Upon scoring a snail or other buried morsel, the snipe's rasplike tongue and serrated bill help move food to the throat. Like hawks and owls, snipe regurgitate pellets of indigestible material.

Snipe lose some of their secretive shyness in spring, when males *want* to make their presence known. Listen at dawn and dusk for an eerie *wuwuwuwuwuwuwu,* created by air rushing through the snipe's outer tail feathers as he dives through the air. Courting males may fly 100 yards or more up in the air before beginning the 25- to 35-mph dive. Their rowing wings interrupt air flow, causing the tremolo sound effect.

When not *wuwu*-ing, males also fly upside down and perform aerial somersaults. A male will mate with any female who enters his territory. Females are initially promiscuous but settle down when a nest site is selected, usually under protective shrubbery or in tall grass. Before she's finished, the female will have scraped out 4 or 5 shallow ground nests, lined with fine grass and shaped with her breast. After the 4 precocial chicks leave the nest, mother and father divide the brood and tend them separately. **G, Y, T, R**

TRUMPETER SWAN

Of wild swans, John J. Audubon wrote, "I have more than once seen them, and you will feel, as I have felt, happier and freer of care than I can describe." Audubon may have even written those words with his favored writing implement: a quill pen made from the primary feather of a trumpeter swan.

Hunted to near extinction in the Lower 48, the last 60 trumpeters south of the Canadian border found refuge in the Greater Yellowstone Ecosystem. A pair of lakes and their associated wetlands in southwestern Montana were ground zero for the recovery effort. Red Rock Lakes Wildlife Refuge was established in 1935 for the express purpose of protecting the remaining trumpeters. Because swans can find open water there all winter, the refuge remains one of the most important nesting and wintering sites for trumpeters in North America. The Rocky Mountain resident population now numbers about 500, and birds from Red Rock Lakes have been used to reintroduce swans in 5 states. Resident birds are joined each year by trumpeters migrating from Canada, pushing the number of wintering swans to 1,500 or more.

Weighing 20 to 30 pounds and standing about 4 feet tall, *Cygnus buccinator* is the largest of all North American waterfowl. And with its 8-foot wingspan, the trumpeter is one of the largest birds in the world to migrate long

Trumpeter Swans

distances. Adults might consume their weight in food every day, eating aquatic vegetation, tubers, invertebrates, and some grains and seeds.

Trumpeters select a lifelong mate when they're 2 to 3 years old. The courtship is a ballet of slow, synchronized swimming in which the swans dip their bills and occasionally blow into the water. After mating, new pairs spend 2 to 5 weeks building a nest, while established pairs usually refurbish their nest from the year before. The tops of muskrat houses are favorite sites for the nests, which can be 6 feet in diameter and more than a foot high.

The female, or pen, lays 4 to 6 eggs and does the incubating, although both parents guard the nest site. The male, or cob, is especially defensive—trumpeting, bobbing his head, and quivering his wings at any perceived threat. The downy cygnets can follow their parents and find their own food within 24 hours of hatching. At about 4 months, the sooty gray youngsters are ready to learn

• TRUMPETER OR TUNDRA SWAN •

Two swan species are found in the Rockies: the trumpeter swan (*Cygnus buccinator*) and the tundra swan (*C. columbianus*). The two look nearly identical, but there are ways to tell them apart. Voice can be the strongest clue. Trumpeters were given that name for a reason: their call is a low, trumpeting *ko-hoh*. Tundra swans, which used to be known as whistling swans, have a mellower voice, higher-pitched and wavering.

Tundra swans are somewhat smaller than trumpeters, though size is hard to gauge unless representatives of both species are standing side by side. If you have a good pair of binoculars or a spotting scope, look for a yellow dot on the bill in front of the eye of adult tundra swans. Trumpeters don't have the yellow mark.

to fly. They learn the deep, loud trumpeter trumpet at this time too.

It would have been truly heartbreaking to lose trumpeter swans, considering they've been part of the western landscape for tens of thousands of years. Teams from Montana State University's Museum of the Rockies recently found the remains of a 46,000-year-old trumpeter in an ancient bed of the old Red Rock Lake lake bed. **Y, T**

BATS

More than a dozen species of bats skim through Rocky Mountain summer nights. Look for them anywhere there are night-flying insects to catch, from urban backyards to Pikes Peak.

The little brown bat (*Myotis lucifugus*) is among the most common species of myotis ("mouse-eared") bats found in the region. Typically seen near streams, small rivers, and other open water, this brown, 2-inch bat is also one of the most likely species to be discovered roosting in buildings.

The long-legged myotis (*M. volans*) is one of the area's largest mouse-eared bats. Found in forested areas, this 4-inch, reddish to dark brown bat roosts in trees, buildings, rock crevices, caves, and abandoned mines. Although much about the long-legged myotis remains a mystery, biologists think that, like little brown bats, they hibernate locally during the winter if hibernacula are available. If not, they probably migrate short distances to find suitable mine shafts or caves in which to hibernate.

Begin to watch for bats even before dark, as they emerge from day roosts to feed on moths and other insects over forest openings

> **Bats are the only mammal capable of true, self-propelled flight.**

●

51

or water. Feeding activity may peak 3 or 4 hours after sunset.

Individual bats can live to be 20 years old, but the species itself has persisted 50 million to 60 million years. Evolving from insect-eating animals that lived in trees, bats are the only mammal capable of true, self-propelled flight.

The order of bats is called Chiroptera, meaning "hand wing." Indeed, the leathery patagium, or wing skin, covers 4 fingerlike bones. A stubby, clawed thumb is located on the front edge of the wing. With such a thin wing, bats are less efficient than airplanes or birds in turning forward motion into lift. But they use their greater wing area in a sort of breaststroke to pull themselves up. Bats aren't as fast as birds, but they are considerably more agile in flight. Where birds intercept insects in flight, bats actually chase and capture them.

Bats use echolocation to find and identify such flying prey as mosquitoes and moths. No need to worry about bats flying into you, since their sophisticated sonar allows them to detect and identify objects finer than a human hair. Interestingly, the bat's closest relative, the shrew, also uses some echolocation.

Bats can carry rabies, although there is much debate as to how widespread the problem is. If you must shoo a bat from your house, wear leather gloves and take care not to come into direct contact with it. **G, Y, T, R**

BEAVER

This lumbering rodent has had a profound effect on both the history and landscape of the Rocky Mountain West. Beaver pelts—not gold, timber, or land— were the motivating force for western expansion, spurring the Lewis and Clark expedition and the Louisiana Purchase.

Although beaver populations were depleted in Europe by the 1600s, British admirals, French lieutenants, Revolutionary soldiers, and gentlemen-about-town were still demanding hats made from the felted underfur of *Castor canadensis,* so trappers turned to the New World. Fortunately for the beavers, a new silk-processing machine eventually shifted fashions, and interest in beaver hats faded around the mid-19th century.

With the exception of human beings, this largest North American rodent alters the environment more than any other animal. Beavers' principal mission in life is to ensure the presence of ponds and wetlands for themselves, which subsequently benefits a whole web of other animals, from fish and insects to moose and mountain lions.

Keep an eye out for evidence of the shy creatures wherever there are gently sloping streams near aspen, cottonwood, or willow trees. Besides the obvious dams and lodges, look for teeth marks on gnawed stumps and trees and watch for flooded paths leading from a pond into the woods. Also listen for the warning slap of a heavy, flat tail as the beaver hears you approaching its pond.

Beaver incisors, which never stop growing, are kept honed by incessant gnawing. The 50-pound animals eat bark, buds, leaves, and twigs, and can topple a 5-inch-diameter tree in less than half an hour to get at the luscious top branches; the trunk is saved for construction projects. Some branches may be cached at the bottom of the pond for winter stores, as beavers don't hibernate.

Dams are typically 10 to 50 feet long and 3 to 5 feet high. Lodges may be built either out in the middle of the water or against a bank. The beehive-shaped

> **A 50-pound beaver can topple a 5-inch-diameter tree in less than half an hour.**
>
> ●

freestanding lodges—some over 5 feet high—have special-purpose rooms chiseled into them for drying off, eating, and sleeping. Bankside beaver lodges usually conceal burrows dug into the bank below the surface of the water. On fast-flowing rivers, beavers may forgo the lodge altogether and just dig the burrows.

Beavers are among the few mammals that establish long-term pair bonds. Although courtship is fairly businesslike, pairs are affectionate and extremely loyal. Family units commonly consist of the adult pair plus 2 generations of offspring. The matriarch usually directs construction and maintenance activities and collection of the winter food cache. Older kits help maintain the dam and contribute to the care of younger siblings.

Now protected by game laws and poor fur prices, beavers are reclaiming some of their old territory. Not everyone is thrilled by this, as the industrious rodents can quickly eat their way through landscape plantings, block irrigation canals, and plug culverts to create ponds right on top of county roads. **G, Y, T, R**

BIGHORN SHEEP

With their heavy, curled horns, muscular bodies, and mesmerizing eyes, bighorn sheep embody rugged beauty, making them a fitting animal symbol for Rocky Mountain National Park.

Rocky Mountain bighorn, or mountain, sheep (*Ovis canadensis*) are grayish to medium brown with a creamy white belly and rump patch and a small, brown tail. Ewes weigh about 110 pounds; rams can reach 275 pounds. Both male and female have horns, though the ewe's remain fairly small and only slightly curved. A ram's horns, on the other hand, may curve around into a full curl and measure more than 18 inches around the base and 44 inches from base to tip. Horn tips on older rams are often "broomed," or frayed on the ends.

In the Rockies, look for bighorns at any elevation on cliffs or rocky slopes, in the foothills, or even in grassy areas near highways. Bighorns are more delicate eaters than deer and elk, preferring wildflowers and grasses over twigs and stems.

Sheep often stay in the mountains during the winter, frequenting southwest slopes where blowing winds may keep the ground relatively bare for grazing. They've been described as seasonal drifters rather than migrators, commonly traveling 3 to 9 miles along age-old traditional paths from summer range to winter range. They even use the same bedding areas to rest along the way. An elder member of the band leads the way, having learned the route from previous generations. Ewes go off alone to traditional lambing grounds when it's time to give birth.

Bighorn sheep are considered among the most socially organized of all North America's hoofed mammals. Outside the breeding season, they live in small bands segregated by age and sex. Ewes, lambs, and yearlings band

Bighorn Sheep

• HORNS OR ANTLERS? •

Members of the Bovidae family (which includes sheep, bison, and goats) have horns. Members of the Cervidae family (which includes moose, deer, and elk) have antlers. Both male and female bovids have horns; only male cervids have antlers, except for caribou.

Antlers are basically bones without marrow and are made mainly of calcium and phosphorus. They are shed each winter after the breeding season and grow back in the spring from a bony base on the skull called a pedicel. During their 4 months of growth, antlers are covered in a soft, blood-rich tissue that looks like velvet. Blood vessels supply the antlers— which can grow 1/4 inch a day—with calcium and other minerals. By early fall the bone hardens and the velvet dries; a buck or bull thrashes its new set of antlers on bushes and saplings, scraping off the covering. Age and an animal's physical condition both influence the size of antlers, but there is no absolute formula linking the number of points on an antler with an animal's age. Teeth are a better age indicator.

Mice and other small mammals like to gnaw on shed antlers for the calcium. Some humans also consume ground antlers, which are sold in Asian markets as aphrodisiacs.

Horns are made of keratin, the same protein found in hair, fingernails, hooves, claws, feathers, and scales. The keratin forms a permanent, slow-growing sheath around a bony core. Although both male and female members of the Bovidae family can have horns, the male's are larger and heavier. In bighorn sheep, interruptions in horn growth during the mating season result in distinctive annulus rings on a ram's horns that can be counted to estimate the animal's age.

Horns and antlers are most often used to impress members of the opposite sex and potential rivals—although impressive skirmishes do occur. When threatened by predators, however, animals are far more likely to defend themselves with their hooves rather than their headgear.

The pronghorn antelope is the only horned animal that regularly sheds its horn sheaths, a characteristic that puts the pronghorn in its own, distinct family, the Antilocapridae.

together, while rams collect in groups in which individuals are roughly the same age.

This social orderliness seems to spill over into the breeding season. Ramming battles are highly ritualistic affairs, more like duels than dogfights. The formal challenge begins when two rams approach each other on stiff legs, heads extended. After a weighty pause, one ram may reach out with a straight foreleg and kick the other under the belly—a bighorn slap in the face. They'll drift away from each other; then at some testosterone-cued moment, the rams abruptly face off, rear slightly, and run toward each other on their hind legs. At the last moment they fall forward to add *oomph* to the 40-mph impact, crashing horns with a reverberating *CRACK!* Instead of being followed by a knock-down-drag-out brawl, the rams separate again, turn sideways, and pose motionless for some moments, displaying their horns. This ramming and posing continues until the opponents feel the contest has been decided. The winner gets breeding rights, although sometimes a third ram will mount a receptive ewe while she watches the two prime opponents going at it. Still, dominant males do most of the breeding, sparing a ewe from being pestered too badly, since the females tend to come into estrus one at a time.

The fact that battering rams don't get brain damage is no accident. The 2 bone layers of the double skull are separated by an inch-thick, honeycomblike layer of spongy, shock-absorbing material. Extra-heavy skin on the head also helps hold body and brain together.

People sometimes confuse bighorn sheep and mountain goats since they share some of the same mountain habitat—but goats have straight, black horns and heavy, white fur. Y, R (See Mountain Goat)

BISON

We usually think of bison as Plains animals, but they've been part of the Rocky Mountain ecosystem for millennia. You'll find *Bison bison* in the mountain meadows of Yellowstone National Park, looking perfectly at home.

Tens of thousands of years ago, the ancestors of present-day bison walked to the New World over the Bering Land Bridge. They eventually migrated southeast along major river and mountain corridors, picking their way across high Rocky Mountain passes on their way to the Plains. Bison bones have been discovered along with the bones of bighorn sheep on summits too steep for a horse. In 1878, a bison skull was discovered above 12,000 feet on Hague's Peak in what is now Rocky Mountain National Park. Arapaho Indians knew Thatchtop Mountain, also in RMNP, as the "Buffalo Climb." The Arapaho trapped bison in Long Gulch, near Mount Olympus.

Bison herds are aggregations of smaller groups composed of about 12 animals, including cows, calves, and young bulls. Mature males are often found on the periphery of these matriarchal groups. Both male and female bison have horns, although the cow's are smaller. The fur "robe" and "chaps" of the male are also longer and thicker.

Bison are in the Bovidae family, more closely related to domestic cattle than to any other wild animal. But make no mistake about it, they are not domesticated and can be dangerous if approached; more than a few Yellowstone tourists have been seriously gored. The rut, or breeding season, begins in August, something late-summer travelers should keep in mind. Listen for the roars. Mature bulls can weigh 2,000 pounds and are surprisingly fast and agile.

In a booklet produced by the Badlands Natural History Association, bison courtship has been described as a "tending bond." This involves a rutting bull remaining close to a potentially receptive female and trying to prevent other bulls from approaching her. Once he successfully breeds the cow, he's likely to move on to "tend" other cows. After a 9½-month gestation period, a 40-pound, cinnamon-colored calf is born. Bison calves are among the friskiest of young wildlife.

Visit Yellowstone in late May to catch the play.

Although they look docile enough, bison can be very aggressive. More visitors to Yellowstone National Park have been killed and injured by bison than by grizzly bears. **Y, T**

BLACK BEAR

Grizzly bears get most of the press, but there's a healthy population of black bears in the

Black Bear

• SOME DAYS, THE BEAR EATS THE BEAR •

In the winter of 1997, in an isolated area on the edge of Glacier National Park, a grizzly bear dug a black bear out of hibernation, dragged it off, and ate it. The grizzly tore through a big, 20-year-old slash pile to get at the black bear denned below. This is a rarely observed occurrence, but the slash pile was near the cabin of a professional observer, a wolf researcher, who documented the event.

The grizzly, which would typically enter its winter digs about a month after black bears have denned, may have been in a feeding frenzy called hyperphagia—a single-minded quest for calories that comes on before bears head into their winter sleep.

Rockies. Black bears generally avoid people (though they will certainly visit stocked cabins or compost piles), preferring rough terrain with plenty of dense cover. Perhaps these habits have kept them off the threatened and endangered species lists. Grizzlies were easier targets as they wandered the open country eventually claimed by domestic livestock, crops, cities, and suburbs.

Unlike the grizzly, the black bear evolved as a forest dweller. Ideal black bear habitat includes a large stand of dense timber, good understory, some small clearings, and a few wet meadows with lush grass and berry bushes. With molars similar to pigs', black bears can eat a variety of foods, including sedges and grasses, fruits and berries, the inner bark of trees, eggs, honey, carrion, rodents—and garbage, whenever they can get it.

Ursus americanus is fairly common throughout the forested habitats of the Rocky Mountain region. Look for large piles of scat, rotten logs that have been ripped open, and berry bushes with broken or stripped branches.

You might spot the bear itself grazing on an open slope or in an avalanche chute. If grizzlies are in the area, that much larger bear, *Ursus arctos*, gets the most productive berry patches.

Black bear boars are 2 to 3 feet high at the shoulder and generally weigh 180 to 400 pounds. Sows are generally 120 to 180 pounds. Depending upon the locale and the time of year, black bears can be black, brown, blonde, cinnamon, or even white. They lack the shoulder hump of the grizzly, and their faces are more doglike.

In the fall, black bears excavate or arrange a den in a boulder pile or tree cavity or under log piles, buildings, or shrubs (serviceberry, if possible). Sometimes a black bear just curls up under dense cover and sleeps on the ground. *U. americanus* isn't the digger grizzlies are, so dens tend to be simpler.

Bears aren't true hibernators and therefore don't experience radical metabolism changes as do some other animals, such as marmots. Their temperatures drop only about 12 degrees, and their hearts beat about half time, so they can rouse themselves if they need to. Nonetheless, during the big sleep, a bear may go 200 days without eating, drinking, defecating, or urinating—and a female may give birth. A pregnant sow delivers 1 or 2 sightless, hairless cubs weighing less than 1 pound while in hibernation. She groggily chews the cords and then goes back to sleep. The cubs nurse quietly, growing big enough to emerge as furry cubs in the spring. Cubs stay with their mother until they're nearly 2 years old.

Black bears often shed a calluslike layer off their foot pads during hibernation, developing new pads that harden in the spring. They also shed 20 percent to 27 percent of their body weight.

Even though black bears would rather flee than fight, they

can be every bit as dangerous as grizzlies, especially when cubs are involved. **G, Y, T, R** (See Grizzly Bear)

BOBCAT

Bobcats are the most widespread wild feline in the Rockies. They're most common in the region's coniferous forests and in the broken, rocky terrain of foothills, but the 15- to 35-pound, long-legged, bobtailed cat with the reddish brown, spotted coat will use nearly any habitat type that offers cover, prey, and privacy.

Your best chance of seeing a bobcat is in winter, when snow forces the cat onto game trails or roads, or in the late fall, when dispersing juveniles are roaming in search of territories. Also keep an ear out: bobcats are fairly vocal and can sound like house cats with very deep voices.

The reclusive *Felis rufus* maintains a mostly nocturnal lifestyle. Wildcats are well suited for nighttime prowling, with eyes that can adjust to very low light and a keen sense of hearing especially sensitive to the high-pitched sounds of mice and other small rodent prey.

As do other cats, bobcats need a higher-protein diet than most other mammalian carnivores. They rely heavily on small rodents to fulfill this requirement, but the opportunistic predators will eat nearly any small animal, including chipmunks, tree and ground squirrels, hares and rabbits, porcupines, small birds, amphibians, crayfish, and deer.

Except during breeding season and while rearing young, bobcats are generally solitary. Mating usually takes place in late February and March, with male and female consorting only long enough to breed. A litter of 2 to 3 kittens is born 60 to 70 days later. The kittens' eyes are blue when they open at about 10 days old, but turn yellow as the youngsters mature. When kittens are about 2 months old, the mother begins to bring them live mice on which to practice their pouncing skills. Kittens remain with their mother into the fall, but set out on their own at about 9 to 11 months of age.

The size of home ranges and the animals' degree of sociability depend on things such as population density, the availability of prey, weather, and the presence of suitable dens or shelters. Bobcats mark their territories with feces, urine, and anal gland scent secretions. Look for the odoriferous deposits, visually enhanced by scrape markings. **G, Y, T, R**

COUGAR

On the way back to the trailhead after a hike, you are thrilled to find a cougar track—until you realize the track is square in your own boot print. There are many stories of *Felis concolor*—cougar, mountain lion, puma, panther, catamount (cat of the mountain)—following hikers, hunters, and other outdoors-

---

• TEETH FOR THE JOB •

Having a variety of specialized teeth–incisors, canines, premolars, molars– is unique to mammals. Deer, wolves, beavers, whales, and humans are all mammals, but each family has its own custom set of chops. Carnivores such as the cougar have the greatest selection of teeth in one mouth. Incisors, the front teeth, are for biting–useful in taking down prey. The long canine teeth are good for tearing meat, and sharp premolars and molars ("cheek teeth") work well in crushing bone to get at nutritious marrow.

Herbivores such as deer and elk have spadelike incisors on their bottom jaw and a hard, toothless pad at the front of their upper jaw. Vegetation is clenched between the teeth and pad and pulled rather than bitten. On the herbivore's lower jaw, a long gap between the incisors and premolars, called the diastema, gives the tongue room to mix food with saliva. Upper cheek teeth are ridged and the lower ones grooved to increase grinding capacity.

people. Some people who have been followed feel that the cats are merely curious about who's moving through their territory.

Normally, cougars would rather keep humans at a distance than confront them. In the last 100 years, about a dozen people have been killed by cougars in the United States and Canada. (Dogs kill about 20 people *each year* in our country and injure thousands more.) Joggers and children between the ages of 5 and 9 seem to be at greatest risk of triggering the cat's powerful predatory instinct; in the summer of 1997, a 10-year-old boy hiking ahead of his family on a well-traveled trail in Rocky Mountain National Park was attacked and killed by an 88-pound lion. The cubless female was tracked down and destroyed. Fortunately, such tragedies are rare.

Chances are you'll never see a mountain lion, even if you want to. But stay alert, especially in rocky areas where deer, their primary prey, are also found. Lions prefer rimrock country with plenty of brushy cover, but they're also found in woodlands, forests, deserts, and wetlands. Their primary habitat need, besides prey, is cover, since they rely on stealth in hunting. Cougars knock down quarry with one quick strike, preferably from above, and dispatch their target with a well-placed bite to the back of the neck.

Cougar

Felid collarbones are good shock absorbers and are designed to provide dexterity to the front limbs. This is why cats can wrap their arms around trees and deer—and explains why cats are better than dogs at batting toys.

Cougars once ranged across the entire United States, but except for a nearly extinct population in Florida and rumors of eastern cats, cougars are now found only in the West, where populations appear to be generally stable and, in some cases, growing. Biologists estimate that between 10,000 and 50,000 roam through the 12 western states. As humans, pets, and livestock move into habitat once occupied by lions and deer, cougar encounters will become more frequent. **G, Y, T, R**

COYOTE

The coyote's yips and yodels bank off canyon walls and waft over open meadows, stringing one corner of the night to another and turning the Rockies into a big sound stage. Although the wide-ranging *Canis latrans* doesn't belong exclusively to the West, it is one of the region's most charismatic and controversial animal icons. Look for coyotes in nearly any habitat at any elevation, but especially on intermountain prairies or in meadows near farms and ranches.

The quick-witted, resourceful, and seemingly ubiquitous canine has inspired a multiplicity of names and stories. He is Old Man Coyote, Medicine Dog, Song Dog, Little Wolf, and Brother. He is hero, villain, wise man, coward, and lecher, all wrapped up in the same, grayish brown fur coat. Some stories credit Old Man Coyote with creating the world. Others tell how Coyote introduced death, after pointing out to the chief's council that this little world isn't large enough to hold all of the people. If everyone lived forever, there wouldn't be enough food. As the story goes, Coyote closed the door on spirits trying to come back to life on earth, and ever since he has run from place to place, always looking over one shoulder and then the other to see if anyone is chasing him.

Even today, if you flush a coyote while out walking, he's likely to lope off, keeping an eye on you over his shoulder.

Despite the traditional stories of Coyote copulating with everything from ducks to married women, the monogamous coyote forms a lifelong pair bond. Social life is structured around a mated pair with pups. Where coyotes are abundant, the pack may also include nonbreeding adults from previous litters that help protect the territory and care for the newest 4 to 7 offspring. Pups are ready to follow their parents and learn how to hunt at about 8 to 9 weeks.

The coyote's primary prey are rabbits, mice, and other small rodents. Watch for coyotes mousing—jumping and pouncing as they go about their business of rodent control. The 30- to 50-pound canines also eat carrion, berries, fallen apples, grasshoppers, and a variety of other edibles. The controversy arises with "other edibles." Coyotes will kill domestic livestock, particularly sheep and lambs, and seem most likely to cause trouble during spring and early summer, when young livestock is available and coyotes have pups to feed. A study done in Colorado found that coyotes kill 5 percent of the domestic sheep flock there. Another study showed that, depending on location, human-caused mortality of coyotes ranged from 38 percent to 90 percent. Even in the face of organized control programs, the coyote continues to learn, adapt, and expand its range and numbers. **G, Y, T, R** (See Wolf)

DEER

An old saying goes, if a pine needle falls in the woods, the eagle sees it, the bear smells it, and the deer hears it. That holds

• MULE DEER OR WHITETAIL? •

Both mule deer and white-tailed deer live in the Rocky Mountain region, and telling them apart is largely a heads-and-tails proposition. Whitetails have smaller ears than mule deer, whitish eye rings, big tails that wave like white flags when they run, and antlers that branch off one beam like a rake. Mule deer antlers branch and then rebranch, like a tree. Also, whitetails don't stot, are a warmer tawny brown, and are more likely to be found in heavy, brushy cover.

true in spades if the deer is *Odocoileus hemionus*—a species Lewis and Clark referred to as "mule deer" in reference to the animal's large ears. We still call them mule deer, and they remain a treasured presence in the Rocky Mountains.

"Muleys" use a variety of habitats, browsing shrubs and trees, grasses, forbs, evergreen needles, bark, berries, and mushrooms. Some deer remain at low elevations year-round; others spend their summers in higher-elevation forests, meadows, and tundra. Unlike moose and elk, deer don't paw through the snow for food, so snow deeper than

about 18 inches usually pushes them to lower-elevation woodlands or onto windswept sage flats.

Watch for bands of does and juveniles feeding in fields alongside roads. You may be lucky enough to see bucks, but they tend to keep a lower profile, even outside hunting season. Be particularly careful driving near dawn and dusk; hitting a deer is bad news for you and your car as well as for the deer.

Mule deer are grayish brown with a dark forehead and white throat, white rump patch, and short, black-tipped tail. Does average 150 pounds; bucks average twice that and can weigh up to 400 pounds. The bucks shed their antlers each year and grow a new set; females don't have antlers.

When muleys are alarmed, they spring away in a 4-footed pogo leap called a stot. This pogo-stick getaway is slower and may be less energy-efficient than running, but biologists think it could be the deer's best way of evading predators. They can bounce right over brush or deadfall that a pursuer would have to scramble through or around, and can change direction in midstot.

There are basically 2 kinds of deer in the United States: black-tailed deer and white-tailed deer. Rocky Mountain mule deer are in the black-tailed group, close relatives to the Columbia blacktail of the Pacific Northwest and the smaller Sitka blacktail of Alaska. White-tailed deer are found throughout the country, including the Rockies, but black-tailed deer occur only in the West. **G, Y, T, R**

Mule Deer

ELK

Fall in the Rocky Mountains is an especially magical time. You can see magic in the sudden gold of aspen leaves, taste it in the soft sweetness of serviceberries, and hear it in the high-pitched call of bugling bull elk—*aaAAEEEEEEEEEeeeee-eough*. The flutey note holds clear and high before crashing down into a series of grunts: *e-UNH! e-UNH! e-UNH!*. Only bulls wail this siren call of sexual desire, and only during the fall rut, or breeding season.

Bull elk bugle to attract cows, warn away other bulls, trumpet their conquests, and because—when fall is in the air—they simply can't do otherwise. Folk wisdom has it that the elk uses special teeth called ivories, or buglers, to make the sound, but in reality the bull calls through his trachea, with his upper lip tight, tongue pushed forward, and mouth cupped. Listen for elk in coniferous forests interspersed with natural clearings or near forest edges facing meadows or alpine tundra.

The elk is the second-largest member of the Cervidae, or deer, family. (Moose are the largest.) Cow elk generally weigh 500 to 600 pounds, and bulls can weigh up to 1,000 pounds, though 660 pounds is a more average weight. Large bulls stand about 5 feet tall at the shoulder.

Considered the most polygamous cervid in the world, a dominant bull elk may collect a harem of up to 60 cows during the rut. Less robust bulls may be satisfied with just a few cows. The rut is an intense time for bulls, which spend the days fighting off challenges, breeding the cows and keeping them in line, and maintaining their sex appeal by wallowing in their own urine and thrashing shrubs and small trees with their antlers. Needless to say, there's not much time for eating, and breeding bulls often enter the winter in a weakened state.

• HOME ON THE WINTER RANGE •

Winter range provides habitat for animals pushed out of their summer homes by cold and snow and is especially important for large grazers such as elk, deer, and sheep. In fact, availability of good winter range is what limits the populations of most big game animals in the Rocky Mountains.

In a natural ecosystem, competition among species is minimal since they seek different types of winter range. Bighorn sheep and elk head for ridges swept clean of snow, or broad, south-facing mountain slopes. Mule deer gravitate to brushy draws, open forests, valleys, or badlands. White-tailed deer seek food and shelter in dense woods or brushy river bottoms.

Since much traditional winter range in the Rockies is now being used for agriculture or development, more and more grazing animals are wintering in sagebrush grasslands such as the National Elk Refuge in Jackson Hole, Wyoming.

Juniper and sagebrush are important food sources in winter, but animals generally can't tolerate more than about 20 percent of those plants in their total diet because they both contain chemicals that, in high concentrations, kill stomach bacteria needed to break down food. Besides the obvious grasses, other plant species important as food to wintering animals include bitterbrush, mountain mahogany, serviceberry, snowberry, currant, and wild rose. Winterfat and saltbush are also important sources of vegetation in many dry, windblown basins.

After the rut, bulls put aside their rivalry and withdraw into their own groups. Depending on the availability of winter range, elk may congregate in large, mixed herds during the cold months. In the summer, cows go back to their matriarchal lifestyle, living in groups of cows, calves, and subadults of both sexes, led by an elder female.

Elk antlers are among the most impressive of the deer family. A yearling bull usually has long, single spikes. In his second year, he might have 4 or 5 "points," or tines, on each antler, but the branch, or "beam," is slender. A 3-year-old may have the same number of points, but be heavier-beamed. Bulls 4 years old and older may have 6 or more points. A bull elk with 7 points on each side is called a "royal," and the rare 8-pointers are known as "monarchs."

Of the 4 subspecies of *Cervus elaphus*, the Rocky Mountain elk (*C. e. nelsoni*) is the most numerous; at least half a million roam the Rocky Mountain region. The other subspecies are the Roosevelt elk of the Pacific Northwest, Tule elk of California, and Manitoba elk of Canada. An eastern subspecies went extinct.

G, Y, T, R

GOLDEN-MANTLED GROUND SQUIRREL

This is one of the most common and easily observed small mammals in the Rocky Mountain region—and the most likely to beg a cracker at a picnic wayside. The golden-mantled ground squirrel looks like a big chipmunk minus the facial stripes. It seems to feel quite at home in campgrounds and parks, but is found more naturally on forest edges and in open woodlands, shrublands, and mountain meadows. When left to its own devices (please don't feed the wildlife), *Spermophilus lateralis* eats seeds, berries, wildflowers, insects, eggs, nestling birds, and fungi. Golden-mantled ground squirrels and chipmunks are very important in spreading beneficial fungus spores; by nibbling on mushrooms they ensure the distribution of fungal mycorrhizae, which essentially function as extensions to tree roots.

Like other ground squirrels, such as the marmot, the "golden chipmunk" is a true hibernator. It usually sleeps alone in a relatively shallow burrow that may be 26 feet long, with side tunnels and chambers and multiple entrances. A nest of leaves and grasses is constructed in the burrow. Researchers have found that golden-mantled ground squirrels living at elevations above 9,500 feet are larger and store more body fat than squirrels living at lower elevations.

These squirrels mate once a year, usually a few weeks after emerging from hibernation. A litter of 5 is born about a month later, and the young are nearly 90 percent of their adult size by the time they're 2½ months old.

Golden-mantled ground squirrels are thought to live only about 2 to 3 years in the wild. Coyotes, bears, hawks, eagles, and other predators take their toll, and animals die during hibernation and of disease as well. **G, Y, T, R** (See Fungus Among Us)

GRIZZLY BEAR

The Rocky Mountains hold something rarer and more precious than gold or oil. This land of many hiding places has provided refuge to the last 400 to 700 grizzly bears in the Lower 48. Originally, grizzlies were creatures of the grasslands as well as the mountains. Lewis and Clark first encountered grizzly tracks along the Missouri River, often near carcasses of bison that had died trying to cross the river in winter. In the 1800s, an estimated 50,000 grizzlies roamed across the entire western half of the United States. Today, grizzlies inhabit less than 2 percent of their historical range.

The presence of *Ursus arctos* can now be felt only in isolated areas of Idaho, Montana, and Wyoming— primarily Yellowstone and Glacier National Parks. Once you have experienced the company of bears, you will never forget it.

Despite the fear they can strike into the heart of large mammals, including humans, Rocky Mountain grizzly bears have a less predatory nature than weasels. The omnivorous ursines eat grass, roots, bulbs, pine nuts, carrion, army cutworm moths, and other insects in addition to catching fish, ground squirrels, marmots,

Knowledge and good judgment are your best defenses in bear country. Learn to recognize potential bear habitat and take appropriate steps to stay safe. Fish spawning areas, berry patches, mountain meadows, and the foot of avalanche slopes are all likely spots to see bears. Either avoid those places or be especially alert. Watch for tracks, scat, or overturned rocks, logs, or dirt where bears have been digging for food.

The cardinal rules for safe travel are: Never hike alone in bear country, and always carry pepper spray. When entering densely vegetated areas, make lots of noise. Eliminate food and cosmetic smells. Never approach any carcass, even if you don't see bears around. If you're camping, cook 100 yards away from your tent and hang food on a clothesline between 2 trees, at least 10 feet off the ground and 4 feet out from the nearest tree trunk.

If you do encounter a bear, don't panic. Pop off the safety clip of your pepper spray and back off slowly, facing the bear and talking in a normal tone of voice. Bears often bluff a charge, veering off at the last second. The best, and hardest, response is to stand your ground. Spray when the bear is in range of your brand of spray.

In the event of an attack, recommended defense strategies are different for black bears and grizzly bears. For grizzly bear attacks, get in a fetal position and play dead, face down with your hands covering your head. In the event of black bear attack, experts recommend you fight back, jabbing the bear in the eyes or nose.

According to a brochure published by the Interagency Grizzly Bear Committee, Wyoming Game and Fish Department, and U.S. Fish and Wildlife Service, there is no statistical evidence that grizzly bears are more likely to attack menstruating women. But since bears are attracted to odors in general, it's prudent to minimize odors by using unscented tampons instead of pads. As with all garbage in bear country, don't bury tampons. Store trash in airtight containers and hang as you would food.

and newborn elk calves when the opportunity arises. Up to 90 percent of the Glacier grizzly's diet is plant material. Recent studies indicate that the diet of Yellowstone bears, however, is composed of up to 79 percent meat. Some of that comes from rodents, but researchers think most of the meat detected in scat

Grizzly Bear

studies comes from elk and bison carcasses that bears find. Observers also say the Yellowstone bears seem to be getting better at catching elk calves.

Although grizzlies will climb trees, their long claws are far better adapted to digging for food rather than climbing. The distinctive shoulder hump is a large muscle most often put to use digging out bulbs or burrowing animals. A hungry grizzly has the horsepower to move a boulder weighing hundreds of pounds if it's in the way of food.

Females weigh about 250 to 400 pounds, while males average 300 to 700 pounds— although one Yellowstone ecosystem grizzly tipped the scales at over 1,000 pounds. On all fours, they measure $3^{1}/_{2}$ to $4^{1}/_{2}$ feet at the shoulder. Standing up, a grizzly can be over 8 feet tall.

The size of a grizzly's home range depends on its age, sex, and available habitat. In Yellowstone, male grizzlies have an average home range of 337 square miles, and an individual can travel more than 200 miles in 24 hours searching for food. A female's territory averages 108 square miles. In late fall, a bear digs out a winter den, usually located on a steep slope at a high elevation. Females essentially sleepwalk through the birth of their tiny cubs, which they deliver during hibernation. Cubs nurse, sleep, and grow during the quiet months.

Biologists have seen some evidence that grizzlies may be expanding their range. Unfortunately, there aren't many wild, 100-square-mile chunks of territory to go around. **G, Y, T** (See Black Bear)

LYNX

Once distributed across the northern tier of the United States, the lynx is a dwindling presence in the Lower 48. Among the region's national parks, only Yellowstone can confirm the current presence of lynx. The cats still range through Canada and Alaska in good numbers, but in the contiguous states they can be found only in isolated areas, including along the spine of the northern Rocky Mountains. No lynx have been documented as far south as Colorado since the late 1970s. Depending on who you talk to, there are anywhere from 200 to more than 1,000 lynx living in the Lower 48 states. The gray to yellowish gray, lightly spotted cats weigh about 20 to 30 pounds and have a bobbed, black-tipped tail, distinctive ear tufts, and prominent cheek ruff.

Lynx are creatures of undisturbed wildlands, usually found in forested high country above 9,000 feet. They remain at high elevations even in winter, when their bobcat cousins move to lower climes. With feet like snowshoes and long legs, lynx are suited for hunting in the snow. They're inextricably linked to their primary prey, the snowshoe hare. The lynx needs about 4 hares a week to sustain itself. Researchers report that *Lynx lynx* has about a 36 percent hunting success rate and may kill and cache hares when prey is plentiful. When the hares are abundant, lynx have robust litters of up to 6 young. When hare populations drop, lynx populations drop correspondingly. When hares are scarce, kitten mortality can exceed 90 percent. ʏ (See Snowshoe Hare)

MARMOT

There aren't any woodchucks in the Rocky Mountains, but there are, appropriately enough, rockchucks. No groundhogs, just whistle-pigs. "Woodchuck" and "groundhog" are names for marmots of the eastern United States. The yellow-bellied (*Marmota flaviventris*) and hoary (*M. caligata*) marmots are strictly western species. Glacier Park is noted for hoary marmots, while yellow-bellied marmots are common in the other parks. The stocky, 5- to 10-pound, 14- to 20-inch-long, yellow-bellied marmot may have a yellow tint to its thick brown fur and does indeed have a yellowish belly. Members of the squirrel family, marmots have bushy tails, which they carry down like other ground squirrels instead of over their backs like tree squirrels.

Perhaps instead of "rockchuck," a more suitable nickname would have been "rock potato." Marmots love to lounge. You're most likely to spot one sunbathing on a warm boulder, watching the world go by. It may spot you first and give a chirpy whistle so that you don't think you're getting away with sneaking around. They're most common above 8,000 feet in alpine tundra, mountain meadows, and talus slopes, but yellow-bellied marmots can also be found in foothills, valleys, and even pastures as long as there are a few lounging rocks. The marmot is much larger than the other high-profile alpine rodent, the pika.

Marmots are fairly selective feeders, choosing such delectables as dandelions, cinquefoil, cow parsnip, and bromegrasses. They often crawl on their bellies while grazing, beating down paths through the vegetation.

Although some individuals are solitary, most marmots live in colonies consisting of a dominant male, several females, and their offspring. Social bonds are reinforced through mutual grooming, play, and sniffing one another's cheek glands.

When they're not eating, sunbathing, or sniffing cheeks, rockchucks are sleeping. They spend an estimated 80 percent of their lives in excavated burrows, 60 percent of that time in hibernation. Most dens are situated on northeast- or southwest-facing slopes near rock outcrops. Front- and back-door shafts lead 2 to 3 feet straight

Marmot

down to a long, main tunnel off which are sleeping rooms and a toilet room. In summer, marmots may use the burrows to escape the heat, going into a temporary summer dormancy called estivation. The winter hibernation begins in September, when rockchucks plug the den entrance behind them and don't emerge until March or April. The animal's normal body temperature of about 100°F drops to just above freezing. Its heart beats about 4 times per minute, and the slumberer takes only 1 breath every 5 minutes. If its body temperature drops too low, the marmot wakes up, shivers to get its blood flowing, and may get up to grab a snack from the food cache and go to the bathroom. **G, Y, T, R**

MARTEN

The marten, also known as the pine marten or American sable, is among the most luxurious-looking little mammals in the Rockies. *Martes americana* is a shy, long-bodied creature smaller than an average house cat, ranging in color from black to orangish brown, with an orangish cream throat and chest. Its legs and long, fluffy tail tend to be darker than the rest of its body.

Martens are in the Mustelidae family—a group that includes fishers, wolverines, and river otters. Unlike most other members of the family, martens spend a good deal of time in trees. Like squirrels, they can rotate their hind feet and walk down a tree headfirst. In summer, they may sleep in the hollows of trees, in abandoned squirrel nests, or in hollowed-out witch's broom.

Look for marten tracks in old-growth or mixed-growth forests of spruce, fir, or lodgepole pine. The marten has 5 toes on the rear paw, but only 4 may register in a track. In winter, the marten's foot is so furry that toe prints may not show. This is true for many animals, making track *patterns* an

Marten

Voles and mice constitute the largest portion of the marten's diet; tree squirrels, chipmunks, ground squirrels, rabbits, hares, and shrews are also hunted. Martens are flexible, hunting during the day, when day-active prey are around, and at night, when pursuing flying squirrels or snowshoe hares.

important factor in identifying tracks in the snow.

Biologists say that a forest with a canopy cover of 40 percent to 60 percent is the best marten habitat. Some also say that moderate timber harvesting and wildfire may enhance certain habitats for martens by opening up a too-dense canopy. This allows for the growth of understory vegetation, which in turns results in the presence of more prey.

With about 4 percent body fat, martens are among the leanest of all wild animals and don't build enough fat reserves to hibernate. In order to survive the winter, they spend a good deal of time

• THE SUBNIVEAN SCENE •

If you had x-ray vision, a quiet field of snow would appear as a network of tunnels, with voles, mice, shrews, and other small mammals going about their business.

Just 6 inches of snow can protect this subnivean world from all but the most extreme temperatures, keeping the ground within a few comfortable degrees of freezing.

Tunnels appear to be excavated after every snowfall while snow is still easy to dig through. Voles dig nearly vertical shafts to the surface and keep them open throughout the winter. The purpose of these shafts isn't certain, but they probably vent the tunnel system and perhaps serve as escape routes.

Both voles and mice sometimes venture out onto the snow's surface at night for unexplained reasons, traveling up to a quarter mile. Without heavy fur or down, the small creatures get cold above the snow, so while on these forays they dig little tunnels along the way to dive into for warmth and perhaps to escape predators such as owls or foxes. Look for warming tunnels and ventilator shafts on winter walks. And as snow melts, you'll be able to see traces of tunnel networks in the snowpack.

In places, heat from decaying ground litter melts the bottom layer of snow, creating a space between ground and snowpack, providing subnivean citizens easier access to such foods as insects, worms, bark, seeds, and vegetation. When all the snow has melted, see if you can detect trails of chewed grass.

During the winter, martens and smaller weasels specialize in hunting subnivean prey and also find shelter under the snow. The slim, agile weasels can easily slip through vole tunnels, while martens gain access to subnivean prey through piles of downed, woody debris or other natural entries such as the space around bushes. Owls, foxes, and coyotes don't infiltrate tunnels, but they do listen for sounds under the snow and pounce accordingly.

hunting and resting under the snow, accessing the subnivean (under the snow) world via natural passageways provided by downed trees or underbrush. Subnivean access may possibly be one of the most crucial needs of this animal, and research has linked martens to old-growth habitat because of the ready access to subnivean hunting and resting sites. Staying under the snow also provides protection against predation by great horned owls, goshawks, lynx, mountain lions, and coyotes. **G, Y, T, R**

MOOSE

If you spot moose tracks or "nuggets" (date-shaped droppings) while out and about in the Rockies, the moose who left them is probably still within 3 miles. Although Rocky Mountain moose aren't considered territorial, they do tend to stay within established home ranges. The moose's home habitat will have a pond, lake, or other wetland to supply aquatic vegetation to eat in summer, and stands of willows or aspen to provide twigs for winter food. Anywhere you might find beavers, you're also likely to find moose.

In fact, beaver ponds are some of the best places to look for *Alces alces.* If you don't see moose at first, wait a few minutes; they can stay underwater for up to 4 minutes grazing on submerged plants. Moose will also use heavily forested areas for cover and to escape the heat and biting bugs of summer, so keep your eyes open in the coniferous woods too.

Moose are the largest member of the Cervidae (deer) family. The Rocky Mountain subspecies, called the Shiras, or Wyoming, moose, is somewhat smaller than the Alaskan moose, but *A. a. shirasi* bulls can still weigh 1,200 pounds and be 6 feet tall at the shoulder. Named after naturalist George Shiras, Shiras moose are native to the Rocky Mountain region north of Colorado; before their intro-duction to Colorado in 1978, moose were only occasional visitors to that state.

Special adaptations have made it relatively easy for moose to muck about in ponds and deep snow. Large, spreadable, 2-toed hooves, and dewclaws that give the foot even more surface area keep the large-bodied animals from bogging down. Their legs are built to move like pistons, with a lifting step that saves energy while traversing marshes or post-holing through snowdrifts. Those legs are also incredibly long for wading

and keeping the moose's body above all but the deepest snow.

Moose are typically solitary animals, though they may share good feeding grounds. Also, bulls will sometimes form reclusive bachelor groups in the spring, when their impressive palmate antlers are growing back. Those

• UNGULATE EXPLAINED •

When you want to impress your friends around the campfire, suggest singing that song about "where the ungulates play." Ungulates are hoofed mammals, including everything from deer and antelope to pigs and horses.

Then if you really want to sound smart, say, "You know, the one with the New World Artiodactyla in it." These are the even-toed ungulates.

There are 8 native artiodactyls in the Rockies, dispersed among 3 families: Bovidae, Cervidae, and Antilocapridae. All are ruminants, meaning they have a chambered stomach and chew their cud. This allows ruminants to eat a large amount of food during a short period of time and then retreat to a safe place to ruminate—to regurgitate, rechew, and digest food at leisure. Cud chewing allows the most value to be wrung from even marginally nutritious forage.

In the Bovidae family are bison, bighorn sheep, and mountain goats. Domestic sheep and cattle are also in this family. Bovids have horns, present on both sexes, which are not branched and do not shed.

The Cervidae family includes deer, elk, moose, and caribou. Cervids have branched antlers, usually present only on the male, and shed annually. Caribou are the only female Cervids to normally grow antlers.

Pronghorns are the lone members of the Antilocapridae family. Both male and female pronghorns have horns, though unlike the bovids, these animals shed their outer horn sheaths each year.

loose groups break up as the rut comes on in late summer, another time when moose become a bit more social. Both sexes are very vocal as they seek each other out. If moose populations are strong, 1 bull may claim a small group of cows, though it's more common for a bull to remain with 1 cow for the few days she's receptive, then move on. The moose rut is far more low-key than the elk rut, in which bulls bugle and wallow and pee and fight throughout the entire season.

Cows sometimes bear twins, but, more typically, a single, 25- to 30-pound calf is born in the spring after an 8-month gestation. Calves stay with their mothers for about a year. Moose look harmless enough, even a little goofy, but cows with calves, or bulls in the rut, are potentially dangerous. **G, Y, T, R**

MOUNTAIN GOAT

Mountain goats are flesh-and-blood embodiments of the alpine environment: white as snow, cool as ice, tough as granite, and beautiful as a clear, winter day in the Rocky Mountains. *Oreamnos americanus* is perfectly adapted for life among North America's summits, saddles, and ridges; no large mammal lives at higher elevations. So accustomed are they to looking out below that the goats' eyes are set in sockets that actually point slightly downward.

One of the most dependable and interesting places to see mountain goats in the Rockies is Walton Goat Lick in Glacier National Park, right off U.S. Highway 2. In spring and early summer, dozens of goats are drawn down from the heights to this unique spot to lick mineral-laden cliffs above a river. Although goats aren't common in the other Rocky Mountain national parks, they are present in scattered locales around the region. Goats have been introduced into the Beartooth Mountains near Yellowstone and into areas of

Colorado, including the Gore Range south of Rocky Mountain National Park. Mount Evans, west of Denver, is another good place to view mountain goats.

Even in winter, mountain goats hold the high ground. They seek out steep, south-facing slopes where wind keeps snow from piling too deeply. If conditions warrant, they'll descend below timberline and find shelter in subalpine forests. The goat's thick coat has 2 layers to protect it from harsh winds and cold. Hollow guard hairs 7 to 8 inches long keep out wind and snow. Under those, a 3-inch insulating layer of soft, woolly underfur traps warm air against the goat's skin. In spring, the goat sheds down to its cashmere long johns. These lords of the mountains look pretty scraggly during the process, but when completely shed out appear impeccably groomed.

The mountain goat's short lower-leg bones and muscular shoulders are designed for navigating up and down rocky

Mountain Goats

mountainsides. Goats are also able to stand with all 4 hooves together on a small spot, opening more options for footholds. A narrow body helps the goat negotiate tight ledges.

Cleverly engineered for maximum traction, each toe of the 2-toed hoof is composed of a hard wall surrounding a fat, rubbery sole. The point of the toe works like a stud on ice, and the pads are great for gripping rock. Toes can also spread apart for better purchase, or pinch together to take advantage of the smallest toehold.

Billies weigh about 150 pounds, and nannies average 120. Both sexes have black, spikelike horns, though the nannies' are smaller. Billies don't butt heads as do bighorn sheep rams; instead, they poke each other in the rear. A special "dermal shield" of skin nearly an inch thick on the male's rump provides protection from the sharp horns. Some Alaska Native groups used this goat skin for body armor. **G**

PIKA

The pika, found exclusively in rocky, mountain environments, may be the most task-oriented alpine mammal in the region. In the late summer and fall, these guinea pig–size, gray-brown rabbit relatives begin clipping and collecting grasses, wildflowers, lichens, twigs, and pine needles, which they lay out to dry for later stacking. By the time winter arrives, an individual pika may have assembled 3 or 4 "haystacks" of cured vegetation, each the size of a bushel basket. Because *Ochotona princeps* doesn't hibernate, it depends on the haystacks for provisions. "Rock rabbits" generally stay beneath the snow all winter, living in the rocky labyrinths of talus slopes— although people report seeing the tailless, big-eared fur balls near ski lifts at some Rocky Mountain winter resorts.

In summer, look for pikas standing watch on boulders or running among the rocks of talus

Pika

slopes, rock slides, and rocky fields near timberline. Also look for their piles of drying greens and listen for the *eep! eep!* of their squeaky-toy voices.

If pikas are among the most task-oriented, they are also among the crankiest small mammals in the mountains. Most researchers make note of the pika's aggressive nature, which is in direct contrast to its cuteness quotient. It follows that pikas are solitary animals, although they do live in loose colonies. An individual's 500- to 900-square-yard territory extends around its hay pile. Perimeters are maintained by rubbing scent onto rocks from cheek pouches and urinating, reinforced by threatening postures and calls, chases, and even fights. Pikas steal hay from one another and are always ready to appropriate the pile of a deceased neighbor. Social interaction occurs only during the mating season. Mothers drive away their young as soon as they're weaned, and adults won't tolerate offspring in their winter rock dens. But the colony shares a warning system of nonstop calls when a predator such as a marten approaches the area. If a weasel appears, however, the pikas know it's best to be silent, as weasels are small enough to enter the pikas' rocky retreats. **G, Y, T, R**

POCKET GOPHER

The term "gopher" is thrown around rather loosely in the West, often used to refer to any ground squirrel, prairie dog, or other rodent that pops its head out of a hole in the ground. But you won't see a real gopher scanning the horizon on a sunny day, as it rarely even ventures above ground.

The plains pocket gopher, *Geomys bursarius*, is most

common in Yellowstone, while the northern pocket gopher, *Thomomys talpoides*, is widespread throughout the other parks. A pocket gopher of any species looks something like a large mole, about 5 inches long, with tiny eyes and ears, powerful front claws curved for excavating dirt, large shoulder muscles for digging, small hips to allow for turning around in small places, and short fur with no nap to allow for easy backup in tight tunnels. Roomy pouches on the outsides of its cheeks, like coat pockets, give this tunneling rodent its name. When excavating, the gopher packs dirt into the pockets, to be dumped elsewhere.

Gophers are not very social and are extremely territorial, meeting only to mate. Females bear 1 litter of 4 to 6 young each year. In summer, the reclusive rodents feed

• EVERYTHING IN ITS NICHE •

In terms of ecology, a niche is more than a physical place—it's the way a species fits into its environment. When 2 species compete for limited resources, the less aggressive population can be forced into extinction. To avoid that situation, many species have evolved lifestyles in which competition with neighbors is limited. Type of food consumed, time of day individuals feed, and the temperature range in which animals can function all combine to create a niche.

If both pikas and marmots stayed active in the winter, the mountain environment might not be able to produce enough food to support both populations. But since marmots hibernate, they use fewer food resources. Also, without winter-active small mammals, predators such as bobcats, foxes, and owls would starve.

Niches seem to be flexible, based more on available resources than on genetics. For instance, in certain coastal areas of Alaska, where weather is relatively mild and food is readily available throughout the winter, grizzly bears may not hibernate.

on tubers and roots, or sometimes whole plants, which they might pull straight down through the ground into their tunnels. Food may be stuffed into the cheek pouches and carried to storage chambers separate from the gopher's den and toilet room. In winter, gophers tunnel through snow to forage for twigs, bark, and other food. Shortly before spring they renew their tunneling in the ground, dumping excavated dirt in the snow tunnels. When the snow melts, dirt deposited in the snow tunnels settles onto the ground, leaving snaky, 2- to 3-inch-wide casts called eskers. Look for the ubiquitous eskers from low-elevation pastureland to alpine tundra at 11,000 feet. In summer, dirt is simply dumped in a fan around the burrow entrance, which the gopher plugs with dirt or sod after it's finished digging.

Pocket gophers have a profound effect on the soil. In areas with large populations (about 74 animals per 2 1/2 acres),

gophers are estimated to move more than 400 tons of soil each year, mixing and cycling organic material and loosening soil to allow better penetration of moisture. On the minus side, if all that soil recycling happens in your alfalfa field, you may not be so appreciative. **G, Y, T, R**

PORCUPINE

The poor, maligned porcupine. It's hard to find anyone willing to stand *near* the loaded rodent, let alone stand up for it. *Erethizon dorsatum* has 30,000 quills, thousands of which end up in golden retriever noses every year. If the nose belongs to your dog, take a moment to appreciate the quills while you pull them out with the forceps you carry in your pack.

The 2- to 3-inch, black-and-white quills are actually specialized, hollow hairs with minuscule, multiple barbs on the black end. You'll notice they pull easier if you cut a bit off the white part sticking out, destroying the vacuum effect.

As you work, the quills are swelling with your dog's body fluids and working themselves in at a rate of up to 1 inch an hour as the dog's muscles twitch. Keep telling yourself that the porcupine did not start the altercation.

Anyone who spends enough time outdoors in the Rocky Mountain region, especially with a dog, will eventually see a porcupine. The 10- to 28-pound animals use a variety of habitats, including coniferous forests, woodlands, and shrublands. In winter, they primarily eat the inner bark of trees, preferably pines, selecting bark from near the top of the tree, where the cambium's sugar content is highest. Look for bright patches of naked trunk high up in the pines; you may even see the porcupine itself, eating or sleeping there. Occasionally porcupines will girdle a tree and kill it, but more often only the top dies and the tree lives on; an upper branch may even eventually bend upward to serve as a new trunk.

Porcupines also eat pine needles, mistletoe, grass, and the leaves of buffaloberry, wild rose, and other shrubs. They eat bones. They also eat brake lines, tires, sweat-soaked ax handles, leather boots, and backpack straps.

It's probably a good thing that porcupines are slow reproducers. After a careful mating, 1 or rarely 2 young are born 7 months later, a long gestation period for an animal of that size. The kit is born in a membranous sac with a full complement of quills that are soft at birth but harden within half an hour. **G, Y, T, R**

PRONGHORN

Though it is among the most exotic-looking large mammals in the Rocky Mountains, the pronghorn is more native to North America than elk or bison. When ancestors of elk, bison, and other mammals migrated to the New World from Asia over the Bering Land Bridge, the pronghorn was there to greet them.

Pronghorns

Somewhat smaller than a deer, the pronghorn is reddish brown with a white rump, white belly and sides, white collar and chest, white cheeks, and a black blaze. Both male and female have horns, though the male's are significantly larger. The black horns curve back like plow handles, with a wedge-shaped point projecting from the front.

Antilocapra americana is not really an antelope, as it's commonly called, but is the only member of its own family, Antilocapridae.

Unlike any other horned animal in North America, the "prairie goat" sheds its horn sheath yearly, after each fall breeding season. New keratin sheaths form, like hooves or fingernails, over the horn's bony core.

A beautifully adapted animal of open spaces, the pronghorn is built for speed. Its legs are narrow and lean, and there are no dewclaws above the 2-toed hoof. The bones of these 75- to 130-pound ruminants are stronger than the bones of cows, allowing them to withstand the impact of a sustained, full-out run. It's interesting to note that pronghorns have been clocked at speeds over 60 mph. This is faster than any predator now roaming North America, and apparently fast enough to outrun the cheetahs with which pronghorn shared the Great Basin in the Pleistocene epoch.

Pronghorns have huge eyes and tremendous eyesight, allowing them to see danger in plenty of time to flee. When alarmed, a pronghorn flares the bright white hair of its rump patch as an extra alert to the rest of the herd. They are terribly curious animals, however, and early hunters used to lure pronghorns into arrow or black powder range by lying on the ground and waving bits of bright cloth.

Evolving in a prairie landscape of no trees, and therefore no deadfall to jump, pronghorns are at a loss when it comes to fences. They can long-jump, but they can't leap over obstacles with any height, so they have learned to scoot *under* fences.

Bucks and does stay together in bands year-round, though during the fall rut the dominant buck gathers in his harem of does and drives away subordinate males. Twins are common, and the doe bears each one at a different location. During the first few days, she leaves them alone for long periods of time and tends them separately to reduce the threat of losing both to predators. In about a week, the fawns are fairly accomplished short-distance runners. In another week, they can run well enough to join the herd. **Y, T**

RED SQUIRREL

You'll know when you enter a red squirrel's territory. Trespassers are soundly scolded with rapid-fire chattering, often punctuated by squeaky outbursts that seem to lift the squirrel right off its feet.

This small, reddish chatterbox with a bushy tail is the Rocky Mountain region's most common tree squirrel. Look for *Tamiasciurus hudsonicus,* also known as the pine squirrel or chickaree, during the day in evergreen forests or aspen patches from the foothills to 12,000 feet; it will probably be sitting on a tree limb 10 to 20 feet overhead, giving you what-for.

When you run into a tree squirrel, look around the bases of the trees for mounds, or middens—residue from years of cone collecting. In a single good year, one squirrel can collect and store 16,000 cones. Middens are inherited from one generation to another and can occasionally be over 30 feet across. Inside the mound of cones, stripped cores, flakes, needles, and seeds, the squirrel excavates a network of tunnels leading to various storage chambers. New cones are stashed there, as well as mushrooms, which the squirrel has first dried in the crotch of a tree branch.

Cones are harvested in the fall while still sealed shut. Unlike chipmunks, mice, nutcrackers, and insects, which must wait until the cones open to get the seeds, red squirrels have cone-cracking teeth.

Half of the cached cones may be eaten in the winter (red squirrels don't hibernate), and the rest remain in the midden as a hedge against future lean years. When left lying out on the ground, cones lose their viability, but in the cool, moist environment of the midden, stashed cones remain viable for several years. Nursery workers and foresters sometimes harvest cones from middens for seeds to use in reforestation.

Other animals also benefit from the chickaree's cone obsession. In Yellowstone, grizzly bears commonly raid squirrel middens for whitebark pine nuts. Middens are important to martens too. Tunnels through the mounds, which are often piled up against fallen logs, provide martens access to underground or subnivean spaces, where the marten's primary prey, mice and voles, can be caught. Martens also use the middens for resting places or dens and may bear young in active middens, where the often-nocturnal martens only occasionally run into day-active squirrels. Martens eat a few red squirrels, but the feisty chickaree can defend itself in most encounters. **G, Y, T, R**

SNOWSHOE HARE

Snowshoe hares' busy tracks lend a sense of liveliness to the snowy quiet of the Rocky Mountain backcountry. By day, hares lie low in scrapes called "forms," concealed in the underbrush. They venture out at night, maintaining a network of escape tunnels through brushy vegetation.

Lepus americanus is widespread throughout the Rockies, particularly in the northern ranges. Most commonly found in willow thickets, snowshoe hares also like to hide in brush patches in or near coniferous forests to over 11,000 feet.

Cued by the shortening days of fall, snowshoe hares (also called varying hares) shed their brown coat, and a white one grows in, perfect camouflage for life in the snowy mountains. If the snow is late, however, you may see a disconcerted white hare rushing worriedly across the brown grass. But once snow is on the ground, the bright white hare with the big, snowshoe feet is totally in its element. The hare's winter diet is composed mostly of evergreen needles and bark, though a more plentiful summer diet includes foliage, twigs, bark, grasses, and forbs.

Although hares are generally solitary, the 10- to 15-acre territories of males and females may overlap. Males tend to dominate in the winter, with females becoming more dominant during the early spring to early fall breeding season. Courtship

• RABBIT OR HARE? •

Rabbits, including the mountain cottontail, are born naked and with their eyes closed, often in a burrow nest that the female has lined with fur, grass, and weeds. Although the young are helpless, mothers may allow up to 30 hours to go by between feedings. Unlike hares, rabbits use burrows and tunnels for raising young and as escape routes.

Hares are generally larger than rabbits, with longer legs and ears. Jackrabbits and snowshoe hares are the Rockies' most common hares. Young hares, called leverets, are typically born in a shallow, fur-lined depression called a form, located under dense shrubs. Born fully furred and with their eyes open, leverets are ready to run almost immediately.

Rabbits may be out at any time of day, but are especially active around dawn and dusk. Hares are primarily nocturnal.

gets a little wild, with hares thumping the ground with their hind feet and having boxing matches and high-speed chases that sometimes end in spectacular tumbling acts. Hares generally aren't vocal, but may scream when in trouble. During the reproductive season, females have 2 or 3 litters of 3 or 4 young. Gestation is about 5 1/2 weeks, and the leverets are born in an unlined depression in the ground.

Snowshoe hares are noted for their dramatic 10-year population cycles. These population booms and busts have a significant influence on the populations of predators that rely on them for winter food. Lynx, fishers, and owls all prey on the 2- to 4-pound mountain-dwelling hares. In fact, the fate of the lynx is closely tied to snowshoe hares in cycles that aren't completely understood. **G, Y, T, R** (See Lynx)

WOLF

Once upon a time, wolves were more numerous in the Rockies than coyotes. Today, the wolf has been eliminated from all but a tiny fraction of its range, but the story isn't over. Gray wolves, *Canis lupus occidentalis*, are repopulating areas of the northern Rocky Mountain ecosystem on their own, and with a little help from their human friends.

Because they were seen as a threat to livestock, wolves were systematically eliminated from the West. Wolves were shot freely as varmints and, in the 1920s, government-sponsored control programs finished off populations in Glacier and Yellowstone National Parks.

A half century later, in the early 1980s, Canadian wolves moved south on their own to recolonize Glacier National Park and, later, other parts of western Montana. In 1995, after a bitter, decade-long debate, 29 wolves were captured in the Canadian Rockies of Alberta and released in Yellowstone National Park and in the wilderness of central Idaho. The following year, 36 more Canadian wolves were trapped and relocated to Yellowstone and Idaho. By 1998, counting both naturally populating and

Wolves

95

reintroduced wolves and their offspring, over 200 wolves lived in the Rocky Mountain region.

Gray wolves (which might be gray, black, white, or tawny brown) have a highly developed social order that revolves around the pack, which typically includes 2 to 8 members. Body language is one means of communicating complex social messages, and the wolves' throaty, musical howling is another important means of communication and expression. Each pack has an acknowledged leader, the dominant or "alpha" male, who may weigh up to 175 pounds. He and his mate, the alpha female—who is dominant over other females—are often the only wolves in the pack to reproduce. Pairs are thought to stay together for many years. Dominant animals usually get the choicest food, have first selection of resting places, and often show

• WOLF OR COYOTE? •

The biggest clue as to whether that shadow you see slipping across the road is a wolf or coyote is your own location. In and around Yellowstone and Glacier National Parks and in the wilderness of central Idaho, you may be seeing a wolf. But elsewhere in the Rockies, it's probably a coyote, especially if the animal is mousing or traveling near a road.

Wolves are much larger and stouter than coyotes. An adult wolf usually weighs over 50 pounds, whereas the typical coyote weighs less than 40 pounds. Still, size isn't the best indication, since some coyotes can appear quite large when seen alone.

Color is an important key. Coyotes are nearly always some shade of tawny gray, while wolves can range from black to tawny to white.

Coyotes have a more pointed muzzle, a smaller nose pad, and longer, more pointed ears than wolves. Wolves have longer legs and considerably larger feet. Both canids howl, but their voices are distinctive. Coyotes tend to yip and yodel, while the howls of wolves are deeper and sound more resonant.

leadership in hunting or traveling situations. The pack works together to take down elk, deer, moose, bighorn sheep, or other large prey.

The pack also works together to support the breeding pair, bringing food to the lactating female so she can tend her litter, which averages 6 pups. As the pups become weaned, the mother may leave them in the care of subordinate females so that she can return to the hunt. **G, Y**

WOLVERINE

As the *Peterson Field Guide to Mammals* sums it up, the wolverine is "a wilderness animal." Once found as far south as the Carolinas, wolverines have retreated to less-populated areas of the northern states. They do occur in the northern and central Rockies, but are far from a common sight. Among the region's national parks, only Yellowstone can confirm that wolverines are still present.

The solitary creatures are constantly on the move and need lots of roadless space. A male wolverine's home range may cover over 400 square miles. He will allow females to have territories overlapping his, but no other males may intrude. This is one reason why wolverines naturally occur at one of the lowest densities of any carnivore. Individuals may roam over 18 miles in a single night.

Wolverines are an appetite on 4 legs. They've been known to steal animals and bait from traps, drive grizzly bears off a carcass, break into cabins, and tunnel 7 feet under the snow to find carrion. Even the scientific name, *Gulo gulo,* refers to their gluttonous nature.

Looking like a cross between a skunk and a bear, and known to leave a mighty scent, the 20- to 60-pound animals have earned the nickname "skunk bear." Wolverines are brown to black, with a lighter-toned stripe running from shoulder to tail on either side of the body. The tail is relatively long and bushy; feet are large with semiretractile claws. Because it sheds frost, the wolverine's dark brown fur is prized for hood ruffs and hats.

This largest terrestrial member of the skunk and weasel family, Mustelidae, has a ferocious reputation. But the truth is, wolverines are primarily scavengers, locating a carcass with their acute sense of smell and then ripping into it with jaw muscles strong enough to tear frozen meat and teeth that can crush bones and tear through chain link fences. Wolverines are incredibly powerful for their size, able to drag a whole moose carcass. They also hunt and have been known to take down occasional big game, but prey is more likely to be small rodents, rabbits, porcupines, marmots, fish, and birds. The meat diet is supplemented by the eggs of ground-nesting birds, roots, berries, and other plant material.

On rare occasions adult pairs may travel together briefly in the winter, and individuals come together to mate, but wolverines are normally solitary. Females may come into season anytime from late spring to early fall. Through a mechanism known as delayed implantation, common to a number of mammals, females can delay implantation of the embryo, so even spring breeders don't begin active gestation until late winter. About 35 days after implantation, a litter of 2 or 3 kits is born in March or April in an unlined den under a brush pile, rock pile, or tree roots. Kits are born helpless and covered with a fine, yellowish white fur, but mature quickly and are able to leave the den at about 13 weeks of age. Y

• F I S H ,   R E P T I L E S ,

&   A M P H I B I A N S •

CUTTHROAT TROUT

When Sacajawea was a baby, cutthroat were the most abundant trout in the Rocky Mountains. Maybe she helped the Lewis and Clark party catch the first one they saw, in the headwaters of the Missouri River in western Montana.

Cutthroat trout (*Onchorhynchus clarki*) live in the cold, clean water of tiny mountain streams, large rivers, and lakes. The flashy, silvery fish have irregular black spots on their backs and tails, and distinctive orange slash marks on either side of their jaws that give them their name. They average

Cutthroat Trout

about 10 inches, but can grow to 18 inches in the right circumstances. Unlike salmon, trout don't die after spawning.

Today, native cutthroat are the minority species. Rainbow trout (*O. mykiss*) take to hatchery rearing much more readily, so rainbows dominate available habitat. Once likely numbering in the millions, native cutthroat trout must now be counted in the thousands. Although rainbows are native to Idaho and extreme northwestern Montana, most of the rainbows now plying the waters of the Rocky Mountain West can trace their roots to hatchery programs. Rainbows are not native to Wyoming or Colorado.

About a million years ago, ancestral trout swam up from the Pacific Ocean into the Columbia and Missouri River drainages. Over time, they adapted so closely to the conditions of different drainages that they split into several subspecies, including the westslope cutthroat of western Montana and the Missouri River drainage (*O. c. lewisi*), the Yellowstone cutthroat of the Yellowstone River system (*O. c. bouvieri*), and the greenback cutthroat of Colorado (*O. c. stomias*). The greenback has teetered on the brink of extinction, but was brought back to the point of sustaining a small catch-and-release fishery in some waters.

The westslope cutthroat, state fish of Idaho, is the major subspecies. Currently found in only 10 percent of the streams they once inhabited, westslope cutts were the piscine stars of Norman Maclean's short story "A River Runs Through It," adapted to film by Robert Redford.

The golden-bellied Yellowstone cutthroat, Wyoming's only native trout, is seriously threatened by lake trout illegally planted in Yellowstone Lake. Aggressive lake trout eat and outcompete native cutts. The implications go beyond fish; cutthroat spawn in streams, providing food for eagles, bears, otters, and osprey. Lake trout stay deep to spawn, removing an important seasonal food source for a variety of wildlife.

Crosses between the cutthroat subspecies, and between cutthroat and rainbow trout ("cut-bows"), are not uncommon. **G, Y, T, R**

MOUNTAIN WHITEFISH

You're sitting on the banks of a lovely river, watching an angler fly-casting. A fish slams the dry fly and begins fighting like mad. The angler smiles broadly, dexterously playing the fish. When the piscine prize is finally drawn to the net, the angler suddenly deflates. It's "just" a whitefish.

The angler must not know that whitefish are in the Salmonidae family along with salmon, grayling, and that elusive trout. Besides being great fun at the end of a fly line, whitefish also taste pretty darned good, even with all the bones, and can rival the taste of lox when smoked. They average about a foot in length, but can grow to nearly twice that size, occasionally reaching 4 pounds.

But a person doesn't need to be catching and releasing, or catching and cooking, mountain

• FISH IN WINTER •

Lakes and rivers rarely freeze all the way to the bottom, but ice cover makes light and oxygen critical factors for winter fish survival.

As long as light and oxygen are adequate, fish can stay active all year. Still, many fish head for quieter stretches of water, looking for deep pools in which to lie. Food resources aren't abundant enough in winter to provide fish with the kind of energy needed to fight currents, so they settle into nooks and crannies out of the flow.

Although most aquatic insects are dormant through the winter, some continue feeding on the bottom, providing enough food to sustain fish through the season of ice.

whitefish to appreciate them. *Prosopium williamsoni* is native to the Rocky Mountains and inhabits large, clear, cold rivers. That should be enough to make you love them. Trout and whitefish evolved together and fill different biological niches, so they aren't in competition; that should make trout groupies not hate them.

If you weren't expecting a trout, you might even think the silvery whitefish was primitively attractive, with its large scales and small mouth. Because they eat plankton, mountain whitefish have few or no teeth, even though they'll readily take a fly or bait. If our frustrated angler gently releases the whitefish, instead of throwing it onto the bank like a "trash" fish, the riverine native can live up to 16 years, filtering plankton out of the water, helping keep Rocky Mountain rivers fresh—and providing great sport, especially during the winter, when trout might not be biting. **G, Y, T**

RUBBER BOA

If you're hiking along your favorite Rocky Mountain trail and think someone has put a rubber snake in the path as a joke, look again. Rubber boas look like, well, rubber boas. This small, stout, brownish green snake is a bona fide member of the boa family—1 of only 2 in the United States. And yes, our boas are constrictors, able to put the squeeze on hapless mice, lizards, and birds.

Rubber boas are somewhat secretive but quite docile; look for them in sandy areas along rocky springs, in coniferous forests (including up in the trees), or in the damp grass of meadows, up to 10,000 feet. Our well-adapted

Rubber Boa

Amphibians are born in the water as gilled juveniles and metamorphose into land-dwelling adults. The young of amphibians can be called larval since they are physiologically different from the adults.

Frogs are a prime example of an amphibian. Born as tadpoles, frogs undergo the radical physical changes of losing gills and tail and developing lungs and legs. The metamorphosis of salamanders is slightly less dramatic, at least from the outside looking in. Young salamanders appear quite similar to adults, with the exception of external gills.

Animals that merely spend lots of time in the water are not amphibians. Turtles and water snakes are reptiles, born on land with functioning lungs.

Rocky Mountain boa is remarkably tolerant of cold. Unlike most other reptiles, it may be active in temperatures as cool as 40°F.

The 1- to 2-foot *Charina bottae* is also sometimes called the double-headed snake because its terminal vertebrae are fused, making the boa's hard, blunt tail look like its hard, blunt head. When raiding a mouse nest, the snake sometimes makes a striking motion with its tail to deceive the parental mouse while it eats the young. Rubber boas are also called ball snakes because, while they're pretty brave with mice, they'll coil into a ball, head in, if you pick one up.

Rubber boas are burrowing (fossorial) snakes and spend most of their time underground in old rodent burrows or under leaf litter. Biologists consider them a primitive species since they have 2 well-developed lungs, whereas more recently evolved snake species have only 1 lung. Reproduction is slow; females don't seem to reproduce every year, and when they do, they give birth to only 2 to 8 young. Individuals in captivity have lived over 17 years.

The authors of *Amphibians and Reptiles of Yellowstone and Grand Teton National Parks,* caretakers of the 17-years-and-counting snake, report that "rubber boas usually, but not always, move slowly. We have observed individuals that, when caught in the field, can be wrapped around a person's wrist where they may stay for hours." In the interest of science, no doubt. **G, Y, T**

SPOTTED FROG

Adult spotted frogs may be the most frequently observed amphibians in the Rocky Mountain region. They are present in heavily visited areas, including Yellowstone and Grand Teton National Parks and Jackson Hole, and they have an attention-getting kerplunking habit. Next time you find yourself walking along a grassy stream bank, listen for the splashy *kerplunk* of a spotted frog diving for cover.

The 2 1/2-inch *Rana pretiosa* has bumpy, olive-green skin with black dots and a salmon-colored belly. Adults have fully webbed hind feet and are almost always associated with the cool, permanent water of streams, rivers, marshes, springs, pools, and small lakes. In spring, females lay 200 to 800 eggs in softball-size masses. The masses may be either anchored to vegetation or free-floating on the surface. Eggs are clear at first, but collect algae and other aquatic flotsam after a while. Although they get pretty gunky-looking, this debris doesn't harm the eggs. Depending on water temperature, tiny tadpoles emerge in 12 to 21 days.

Tadpoles use horny ridges on their lips to scrape algae and other vegetation off rocks for food. Hind legs appear in about a month and a half, then the left front leg, followed shortly by the right front leg. The tail doesn't completely disappear until the frog has had time to learn how to hop on land. In the last 2 weeks of tadpolehood, the individual grows larger and basks on the edge of its pond.

Adults may move away from water after breeding, so keep an eye out for spotted frogs wandering through mixed coniferous and subalpine forests, grasslands, and even sagebrush habitats. Spotted frogs eat spiders, ants, moths, snails, mosquitoes, worms, grasshoppers, beetles, caddis flies, and whatever else they can get their tongues on.

In the Yellowstone area, spotted frogs may live to be 10 years old. This is fortunate, since mortality of tadpoles in years of drought or sudden freezes can be almost 100 percent. It's beginning to look like the Rocky Mountain region is becoming a repository of spotted frogs. Although the once-common species may have recently become extinct in Washington and Oregon, *Rana pretiosa* seems to be in decent shape here. Or at least what passes for *R. pretiosa*. Biologists have recently been questioning whether the spotted frogs of Yellowstone and Grand Teton have diverged into a new species. **G, Y, T**

TIGER SALAMANDER

You're going to have to make an effort to see one of these, but it's worth it. At just over a foot long, tiger salamanders are the largest terrestrial salamanders in North America. They live in wet Rocky Mountain forests in the

• SALAMANDER OR LIZARD? •

The difference between salamanders and the similarly shaped but wildly different lizards is night and day. Literally. Dry-skinned, sunshine-loving lizards are out basking whenever there are rays on rocks. But moist-skinned salamanders would shrivel and die if caught out for long on a sunny day. This is why they're most likely to be on the move at night, during or right after a rain.

Generally speaking, you won't find a lizard and a salamander in precisely the same habitat. They may both be in residence on a sage flat, but not in the same spot at the same time.

Tiger Salamander

vicinity of rivers, streams, ponds, and lakes up to 11,000 feet and can also be found near streams in low-elevation sagebrush flats, grasslands, meadows, and even in stock tanks. Generally, you won't find salamanders near water with significant fish populations, probably because fish tend to eat the water-dwelling juveniles.

Look for adults under leaf litter near the water, or go out some rainy, spring night and search for them crawling to and from breeding ponds. *Ambystoma tigrinum* ranges in color from light olive to almost black, with yellow blotches or streaks. Its head is broad and fairly flat, with a large mouth and protruding eyes.

Tiger salamanders eat tadpoles, earthworms, insects, and the occasional mouse. They in turn are eaten by great blue herons, trout, otters, garter snakes, ravens, and other opportunists.

Adults hibernate through the Rocky Mountain winter in abandoned animal burrows or some other protected hibernacula, sometimes far from water. Upon emerging in spring, they head for breeding ponds. As with all amphibians, salamanders are born from eggs laid in the water and metamorphose into land dwellers. Unlike frogs, whose tadpoles look nothing like adult frogs, larval salamanders look like adults, except they have external gills. These gills look like feathery pigtails and disappear as the salamander develops lungs. Some tiger salamanders remain in the gilled state their entire lives. Theoretically this means they're still juveniles, yet somehow these axolotls manage to reproduce.

G, Y, T, R

ARMY CUTWORM MOTH

Cutworm moths do advance like an army, from lowlands and plains, where the caterpillars emerge, to the mountains, where adult moths sip wildflower nectar and provide a midsummer feast for grizzly bears. In the fall, survivors of the grizzly raids retreat back to lower elevations to lay eggs, recruiting more troops for next season's engagement.

Euxoa auxiliaris is a western species whose range centers on the Rocky Mountains. In the spring, ravenous caterpillars eat their way through grassy fields as well as through vegetable gardens, winter wheat, and alfalfa fields. Then they march to the next green pasture—sometimes 150 cutworms per square foot in boom years triggered by wet springs.

After eating their fill, the fat caterpillars go underground to pupate, emerging in early summer as brownish gray moths with a wingspan of about 1 1/2 inches. Locals know these moths as "millers" because their loose wing scales make it appear as though they're covered with a brownish flour. (The wings of all Lepidoptera—moths and butterflies—are covered by minute, fishlike scales.)

If your house happens to be on the migration path, expect to see groups of fat millers clinging to interior and exterior walls or squeezed into door and window frames, where they leave orange

• LEPIDOPTERA LIFESTYLE •

Humans are born; then they basically grow up. After the Lepidoptera—moths and butterflies—are born, they undergo major remodeling before reaching adulthood.

After mating, the Lepidoptera lay their eggs, generally on plants that will feed the emergent caterpillars. Eggs can be laid in clusters, chains, rows, or singly, and may be any of a variety of shapes and textures. Some eggs hatch before winter; others won't hatch until the following spring.

From the egg comes the caterpillar—an eating machine that may increase its weight ten-thousandfold over the course of a month or two. To accommodate this growth, some caterpillars molt several times. Each period between molts is called an instar.

Caterpillars of both moths and butterflies form chrysalides, chambers for the next metamorphosis. Moth caterpillars may go on to spin covering cocoons. Chrysalides can be shaped like curled leaves, thorns, pellets, or pods. Some species spend as few as 8 days in this pupal stage, while others will be years in the chrysalis.

The last, remarkable rebirth is as a fluttering moth or butterfly.

dribbles of sexually attractant chemicals called pheromones. Old, abandoned buildings are another favorite roosting place, and the moths can pour out by the millions if disturbed.

Depending on the availability of other foods, millers can be an important summer food source for grizzly bears. After traveling up to 300 miles to get to the mountains, the moths hide in the cracks and crevices of talus slopes, for reasons yet to be discovered. Bears know this and scoop out the nutritious morsels by the thousands. A study in Glacier National Park has determined that Glacier grizzlies may eat 20,000 to 40,000 moths in a 24-hour period. Millers are half a calorie apiece, so the bears may be ingesting in the neighborhood of 300,000 calories in one month of moth eating.

Moths may become a critical source of food in Glacier. The whitebark pine tree, the nuts of which are a traditional source of food for grizzlies, has been driven essentially extinct there by a plant disease called blister rust, which is not native to this country. **G, Y, T, R**

BARK (or ENGRAVER) BEETLE

They leave their snaky engravings under tree bark like clues in a murder mystery. And they can be accomplices to murder, gnawing their way through a tree's phloem layer until the food and water transportation systems are so debilitated that the tree dies.

Bark beetles are secondary pests, typically infecting a tree already in decline or under stress from other factors. The beetles aren't an exotic pest—they're native to the region—and, in balance, can serve an important role in the Rocky Mountain ecosystem. They keep forest succession going by killing coniferous trees, recycling them back into the soil and letting understory vegetation and saplings have their day in the sun. But years of fire suppression policies have resulted in crowded forests of older, less robust trees. In some areas, bark beetles have proliferated, creating serious infestation problems. Next time you walk through a stand of dead conifers, look on trunks where the bark has fallen away for telltale tunnelings.

Within the Rockies are several species of engraver beetles (family Scolytidae). Each species leaves a distinctive pattern and often associates itself with one particular kind of tree. Adults live most of their lives under the bark, emerging only to find a new host.

The ladybug-size flying female of *Dendroctonus ponderosae,* the mountain pine beetle, burrows her way under bark to engrave 1 or more "brood galleries" in which to lay eggs. When the eggs hatch in 2 weeks, the grublike larvae begin boring their own way

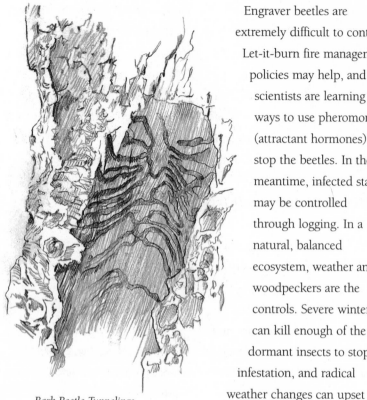

Bark Beetle Tunnelings

Engraver beetles are extremely difficult to control. Let-it-burn fire management policies may help, and scientists are learning ways to use pheromones (attractant hormones) to stop the beetles. In the meantime, infected stands may be controlled through logging. In a natural, balanced ecosystem, weather and woodpeckers are the controls. Severe winters can kill enough of the dormant insects to stop an infestation, and radical weather changes can upset reproductive cycles.

through the inner bark. Besides disrupting the tree's nutrient flow, some engraver species actually carry fungus into the galleries on special mouth structures. The fungus, on which they feed, also holds fluids back from flowing into the galleries, leaving the bark more prone to rot.

Woodpeckers pry away loose bark and consume huge numbers of grubs. **G, Y, T, R**

MAYFLY

In Hawaii the rally call is "Surf's up!" In the Rockies it's "The hatch is on!" The mayflies and the trout are rising.

Often triggered by weather and water conditions, hatches occur sporadically throughout the summer on rivers and lakes. Mayflies aren't the only insect to produce a hatch, but these slender, sail-winged trout temptresses appeal to fish and fly fisher alike. Imitations of mayflies in the various stages of their life cycle are probably the most common fishing flies used in trout waters of the West.

North America has well over 500 species of mayfly in the order Ephemeroptera, which translates as "short-lived, winged insects, enduring but a day." Indeed, adults live only 1 to 2 days, although the entire life cycle takes about a year to progress from egg to aquatic nymph to adult dun (subimago) to adult spinner (imago). The nymphal, or juvenile, stage is most important to fish and fishers. Once the gill-breathing nymph reaches about $1/8$ inch long, trout begin to key on it as food, and nymph-

patterned wet flies are standard in the fly box.

Feeding on vegetation, the nymph grows larger and larger through a series of molts. While it's growing, it's also metamorphosing in preparation for the final day or days of life out of the water. When ready for that first breath of air, the nymph begins to swim toward the surface. It rarely makes it on the first try, swimming up and drifting back in a sort of water ballet. Finally, it reaches the surface and molts one last time out of its nymphal skin. This is the beginning of the hatch. Look for duns floating on the water's surface as their newly unfolded wings are drying. Casting dry flies to trout that are rising to floating duns is a classic fly-fishing experience.

After drying, the dun flutters up, heading for cover on land. It lights on weeds, trees, or your knee as you take a break on the bank. Sometime within the next 48 hours, the mayfly will again

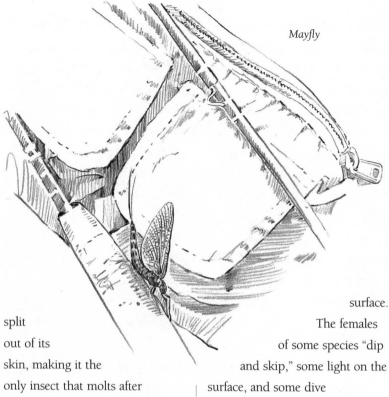

Mayfly

split out of its skin, making it the only insect that molts after functional, adult wings are in place. The reproductively ready spinner looks like a dun with longer, more transparent wings and a more vividly colored body. Males leave their cover and swarm over the water in courtship flight. Females join them, getting caught and mated in midair. When the male releases her, the female lays her eggs on or under the water's surface. The females of some species "dip and skip," some light on the surface, and some dive underwater to deposit eggs. About 1 to 3 hours later, when it's all over, the exhausted insects fall onto the water. Listen for trout slurping them up. Listen for the call "The hatch is on!" **G, Y, T, R**

SNOW FLEA

It's enough to make you itch under your long johns: a zillion snow fleas peppering the snow, bucking like tiny broncos. But don't worry; they aren't really fleas, and they couldn't care less about you or your dog.

Snow fleas are in the Collembola, or springtail, order. These minute, wingless insects have a forklike peg, called a furcula, on their underside, held in tension by a catch. It works like a sort of built-in catapult. Upon releasing the catch, the snow flea flings itself forward or up at great velocity. Try to keep

• FOOD FOR TROUT—AND DIPPERS •

Many of the flying insects you'll see around rivers and lakes in the Rockies have spent more time under the water than over it. Dragonflies, damselflies, mosquitoes, caddis flies, mayflies, stoneflies, midges, and craneflies all spend a significant portion of their life cycle as trout food: gill-breathing aquatic bugs, creeping, swimming, or drifting through the freshwater underworld.

Eggs laid in the water hatch into nymphs, the larval form of the insect. As they grow larger, nymphs repeatedly molt out of their outer skins, or exoskeletons. Besides feeding fish, larval aquatic insects are a significant food source for the dipper bird.

Some nymphs burrow; others crawl or swim. Caddis fly nymphs construct casings of sand or tiny sticks and carry their shelters like hermit crabs.

While growing, nymphs are changing physiologically in preparation for a last hurrah out of the water. The nymphs of some species, including the mayfly, swim to the water's surface to emerge from their shells as flying adults. Other nymphs, including those of the stonefly, crawl out onto a rock or stream bank and split out of their nymphal skin, letting their new wings and skin harden as they crawl farther away from the water toward cover. On rivers with major stonefly populations, the banks can be encrusted with millions of shed stonefly skins.

Typically, the adult, flying portion of these insects' lives is the shortest. Adult aquatic insects may live only 1 or 2 days, just long enough to mate and lay the next generation of eggs.

your eye on one individual—the jump will be so fast that the bug appears to vanish.

Look for snow fleas during a late-winter or spring thaw, when sunshine and warm temperatures draw them up from the soil to the surface of the snow. You may first notice them collecting in old tracks; it will look like someone gave a few liberal shakes of a pepper shaker.

In the Rockies, springtails are most abundant in forest eco-systems, feeding on bacteria, fungi, algae, pollen, lichens, and decaying vegetation and carrion. Even poor soil can support several thousand springtails per square yard. Among the invertebrates cashing in on this ready food source are spiders and centipedes.

There are over 650 species of springtails found in North America. Keep an eye out for some of those other species congregating on the surface of stagnant water or trampolining from bird nests. You might also see them jumping around in your potted plants. **G, Y, T, R**

· T W O ·

P L A N T S

PLANTS

E levation is key in determining which plant species grow where in the Rocky Mountains. Other factors also have an effect—which way a slope is facing, for instance, and the availability of water— but elevation is the dominant influence. Cooler temperatures at high elevations often dictate the upper range of a species, while a progressive reduction in the amount of moisture at descending elevations usually determines the lower range. So basically, each species has an upper limit where it gets too cold, and a lower limit where it gets too dry.

Hiking up a mountainside is roughly equivalent to traveling north on the earth. For every 2,500 feet a hiker gains, a traveler would have to go about 400 miles north, or a little over 10 degrees of latitude. At the end of their respective journeys, the traveler and the climber might see some of the same plants at sea level in the Arctic and at 10,000 feet or so in the Rocky Mountains.

LIFE ZONES

Ecologists have identified 5 major levels, or life zones, in the northern and central Rockies. From lowest to highest, the zones are plains, foothills, montane, subalpine, and alpine. Average temperatures drop a little over 7 degrees from zone to zone, so on a summer day it may be sweaty hot in a low-elevation valley and pleasantly cool just a few miles up the mountainside. It will probably be moister on the mountain too, since precipitation generally increases with altitude (unless you're in the rain shadow on an east slope).

You won't find roadside signs at the edges of life zones. Upper and lower zone limits shift with topography, and since the transition is gradual, zones overlap. Plants and trees often occur in more than one life zone, so look for the combination of certain flora or the clear dominance of certain species when trying to identify a zone. The following descriptions are meant *only* as a general guide. Elevations and precipitation will differ at varying latitudes within the region.

The plains zone receives an average of 15 inches of precipitation a year and can be found up to elevations of about 5,500 feet. Grasses and sagebrush are the dominant plants, but you'll also find juniper trees in dry areas and cottonwood trees and willows growing along streams. Sego lily and prickly pear also grow in this zone.

The foothills zone receives about 20 to 25 inches of precipitation and ranges from about 5,500 feet to about 7,000 feet. This zone includes

ALPINE

SUBALPINE

MONTANE

FOOTHILLS

PLAINS

large, open areas of sagebrush and grass, and forests also begin here. Where it occurs, ponderosa pine is a key tree species. Outside the ponderosa's range, look instead for limber pine, juniper, and Douglas-fir. Aspen grows in this zone in areas where water is abundant. Arrowleaf balsamroot and Rocky Mountain iris are common foothills flowers.

The montane zone ranges from about 7,000 feet to about 9,000 feet, and this zone receives 25 to 30 inches of precipitation a year—enough to support dense, shady forests. Doug-fir dominates here, except in areas kept open by repeated wildfires. Aspen continues into this zone, and Engelmann spruce and lodgepole pine are representative conifers. The montane zone contains open, grassy "parks" interspersed with wooded areas. Look for columbine and Indian paintbrush.

The subalpine zone receives over 30 inches of precipitation each year and extends from about 9,000 feet to timberline, which is typically found at 10,000 to 11,500 feet. Patches of snow may still be on the ground into August. Engelmann spruce and subalpine fir are the dominant trees, and whitebark pine also grows here. Aspens hold on in this zone; look for bent trees marking the path of snow slides. This is also where you'll find krummholz and flag trees—stunted trees shaped by wind and snow. Mountain blueberry and wood nymphs can be found growing in the subalpine zone.

Timberline marks the ecotone, or boundary, between the subalpine and alpine zones. No trees grow in the alpine zone, where tundra habitat dominates with grasses, sedges, and perennial wildflowers. Flowering plants are often compact and fuzzy or grow in mats close to the ground, protected from drying winds. Look for moss campion here. (See also Aspect)

ASPEN

Some people hear the voice of the Rocky Mountains in whispering aspen leaves. As the most widespread deciduous tree in the mountains, aspens interrupt the needle-voiced firs and pines with leafy chatter.

Populus tremuloides has the greatest range of any tree in North America, but is particularly significant in the Rockies, as it's the most common deciduous tree in the montane and subalpine zones. Look for groves of the whitish-trunked "popple" growing along streams or in moist soil from foothills to timberline.

"Quakies," as they're also called, are well adapted for life in the Rockies; the famous leaf-quaking characteristic is one

• TREE OR SHRUB? •

Trees are woody perennials with 1 erect stem or trunk at least 12 feet tall and at least 3 inches in diameter. Trees also have an identifiable crown. Some species, especially certain willows, that reach 12 feet but have several trunks from the same root may still be considered trees.

Shrubs are also woody and perennial, but are smaller than trees and commonly have multiple trunks or stems from the base. There is a great variety of form among shrubs, including tall and bushy, low and compact, prostrate, and creeping—sometimes growing only 1 to 2 inches above the ground.

example. The flat stem of an aspen leaf is set at right angles to the leaf's surface, so the leaf waggles in the slightest breeze— hence the species name, *tremuloides*. This waggling constantly moves the topmost leaves out of the way so that sunlight can penetrate into the tree, allowing the lower leaves an opportunity to photosynthesize. Aspens are thus able to thrive in the short growing season.

As a backup, aspens also have photosynthetic bark (look for the greenish hue), which further allows a small amount of food to be produced when leaves are off

Aspen Grove

the trees. While you're looking for the green hue, look also for scars left by bear claws and elk teeth. Bears may climb aspens or use the trunks as scratching posts, their claw marks eventually turning to black scars on the bark. When elk nibble the bark for food, they leave horizontal scrapings that eventually scar over as black, slightly puffed-out patches. (Fungal infection also causes black trunk markings.)

Another of the aspen's adaptations allows the tree to freeze solid without ill effect. As temperatures get colder, water is drawn out of living cells before it freezes, preventing ice crystals from forming in the cells. As ice melts in the spring, cells suck the water back in, and normal cell function resumes. If a sudden cold snap occurs during this vulnerable state, however, the tree can be severely damaged.

Individual aspens live relatively short lives, typically 80 to 100 years, but the parent organism may persist for centuries. Aspens in the Rockies propagate almost exclusively by cloning themselves. What looks like a cluster of individual trees are actually suckers growing from one horizontal taproot. Because they are essentially one plant, in the fall all aspens in a clone turn the same color at the same time and drop their leaves simultaneously.

Although aspens do produce seeds, they don't seem to germinate well in the Rocky Mountain environment. Some researchers believe that all aspens alive in the Rockies today are direct cloned descendants of trees that grew from seed during the Pleistocene, about 12,000 years ago, when the climate was wetter.

Aspen groves are one of the most diverse ecosystems in the region. Understory plants such as wildflowers, grasses, berry bushes, and wild roses provide food and cover, as do the trees themselves. Bears, elk, deer, foxes, beavers, tree squirrels, weasels, woodpeckers, warblers, ruffed grouse, owls, and hummingbirds are only a sampling of animals that might be found among the aspens. **G, Y, T, R**

CHOKECHERRY

Don't expect the civilized sweetness of a Bing when you bite into a chokecherry—take the name as a hint. Yet for all their pucker, the red-black, blueberry-size cherries make delicious syrup, jelly, jam, and even wine. In times past, this single-pitted relative of peaches and plums (whose fruits are technically called drupes) was a key ingredient in pemmican, the calorie-dense food traditionally made of game meat, fat, and berries.

Prunus melanocarpa is widespread in the Rockies, growing as a large shrub or small tree to about 20 feet tall. In shrub form the plant looks something like a serviceberry, but is typically larger, with lance-shaped, finely toothed leaves 1 to 4 inches long. Look for the lovely, elongated clusters of creamy white chokecherry flowers in May or June near creeks and in moist soils to about 8,000 feet.

Native Americans typically harvested the fruits after the first hard frost, when they seemed to be at their sweetest, or least sour. Women pounded the cherries, pit and all, and formed patties of the mash. These patties were staples among early peoples and found a place in modern times as well. According to *Edible Native Plants of the Rocky Mountains,* published in 1967, chokecherry patties were being traded among certain Indian tribes in 1962 for 50 cents per cake.

Members of the Lewis and Clark expedition ate chokecherries and used the plant

> **Chokecherry patties were being traded among certain Indian tribes in 1962 for 50 cents per cake.**
>
> ●

medicinally. At a campsite on the upper Missouri, Captain Lewis treated his abdominal cramps and fever with a tea made of chokecherry twigs. He reported feeling fine the next day. Mountain man Hugh Glass is said to have kept body and soul together on chokecherries after being mauled by a grizzly bear. With the right advice, Glass could have also used an infusion of the bark on his wounds. Some Indians infused chokecherry bark to cleanse sores and burns and used other parts of the plant to treat an array of ailments, especially gastric complaints.

Certain parts of the chokecherry plant can be poisonous. The pits, for instance, contain potentially deadly cyanic acid. Although Native Americans pounded the fruit—pits and all—for use as food with no apparent ill effect, children in more recent times have reportedly been sickened by eating too many unpitted fruits. The leaves can also be poisonous in spring and early summer, and cases of livestock poisoning have occurred. Still, mountain goats, deer, and elk regularly browse the stems and leaves, and birds and bears eat the fruit without noticeable complaint. **G, Y, T, R** (See Serviceberry)

COTTONWOODS

This member of the willow family grows along streams and rivers, and you'll also see the massive, shady trees growing in long-established yards and parks throughout the region. The cottonwood was the only broad-leafed tree pioneers saw on their way across the Plains, so this was the tree they planted on their homesteads and in their new towns.

There are at least 4 cottonwood species in the Rockies. The narrowleaf cottonwood, *Populus angustifolia,* is a relatively common, higher-elevation species that grows in canyons and near streamsides from the plains up to 10,000 feet. Narrow, 3- to 5-inch-long leaves give this tree a willowlike appearance. The whitish bark is somewhat smooth, but becomes darker and more furrowed with age. This tree is smallish for a cottonwood, growing only to about 60 feet high.

The black cottonwood, *P. trichocarpa*, is the largest poplar of the region, occasionally reaching 165 feet in height and 9 feet in diameter. The tree's thick, gray bark is deeply furrowed. Leaves are 4 to 8 inches long, finely toothed, and roughly triangular. Dark green on top, the leathery leaves show a silvery underside in the wind. When crushed, buds get gummy and release a spicy scent. Female trees produce cottony seeds that give the tree its name and that blow through the air or along the ground like snow.

Like other trees in the willow family, cottonwoods have a relatively short life span, rarely living to be 200 years old.

Indigenous peoples ate the sweet inner bark and sap of this tree. Bark was peeled in the spring, while sap was running, with the aid of a stripping tool made from the rib of a bison or elk. Some tribes scooped out a portion of the trunk in which to collect sap for eating.

Lewis and Clark used cottonwood canoes during their journey. For some reason, Clark rejected the Indian way of making dugouts by burning out the center, and during the construction of two new canoes above Great Falls, his men broke 13 chokecherry ax handles on the first day. Four days later the canoes were ready to launch.

A few decades later, countless cottonwoods would fall to the saws of men who cut and sold them as fuel for the river steamboats. Although it uses and stores lots of water, dry cottonwood makes great firewood, as it produces clean smoke and doesn't pop. **G, Y, T, R**

DOUGLAS-FIR

Douglas-fir is the grandfather tree of the Rockies, a forest-succession climax species that takes over from pioneering aspen, lodgepole pine, and ponderosa pine. *Pseudotsuga menziesii* is the second most widely distributed conifer in the region, behind ponderosa.

In Rocky Mountain habitats, this distinguished tree may live to be 750 years old, reaching 100 feet in height with a trunk 3 feet in diameter. (Doug-firs grow much larger in the moister climate of the Pacific Northwest.)

Shaped somewhat like a pyramid, a mature Doug-fir has thick, furrowed bark patterned in dark and light brown. This is the signature tree of the montane zone, a habitat higher in elevation than foothills and lower than the subalpine zone.

Flat, blunt, ³/₄- to 1¹/₂-inch needles generally radiate out in all directions from the branch. Cones are distinctive, with a paper-thin, 3-pointed bract sticking out from beneath each scale. One old story tells of a mouse that got stuck in a cone while collecting nuts for the

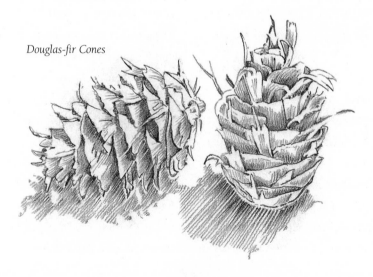

Douglas-fir Cones

winter. Pick up a cone and see for yourself if the bract sticking out doesn't indeed look like the flattened back end of a mouse, complete with tail.

Douglas-fir isn't really a fir. Most botany books hyphenate the name as a way to differentiate Doug-fir from the true firs, such as subalpine fir and grand fir. The tree isn't pine, spruce, or hemlock either, and its closest relatives are in Japan and China.

The tree's common name refers to Scottish explorer and adventurer David Douglas, and the species name is a nod to Archibald Menzies, surgeon and botanist on Captain Vancouver's ships in the late 18th century. **G, Y, T, R**

ENGELMANN SPRUCE

There's a good chance you'll schuss past an Engelmann spruce while recreating at a Rocky Mountain ski resort. *Picea engelmannii* is the dominant spruce of the interior western mountains, forming vast forests in the upper montane and subalpine zones of the region.

The dark green to blue-green tree typically grows 80 to 120 feet tall with a diameter of 1 to 3 feet. Like those of other spruces, the cone of this species has papery scales and hangs down from the branch. The light brown cones may be mostly crowded around the top of the tree. Also like other spruces, Engelmann needles are 4-sided. Bark is thin and scaly and comes off easily; in a survival pinch, collect "spruce dollars" for kindling.

Engelmann spruce is a major commercial species in the West. The wood is used in construction and for pulp, but is also reported to have acoustical properties like Sitka spruce, whose wood is used in crafting guitars, pianos, and other musical instruments.

George Engelmann was a 19th-century St. Louis physician. He had a keen interest in western plants, particularly cone-bearing trees, and traveled widely to study

• ASPECT •

In the mountains, aspect can have nearly as great an influence on habitat as elevation. Aspect is the direction in which a slope faces. This determines the amount of sunlight, wind, frost, and snowpack to which the land is exposed, which in turn affects the types of plants and trees that grow there. Slopes within sight of one another—especially north-facing and south-facing slopes—may be dominated by completely different tree and plant species. Aspect helps create a mosaic of various habitat types, enhancing the plant and animal diversity of an area.

Along with influencing habitat, aspect has also proven to be an important factor in land use. North-facing slopes can be 6°F colder than south-facing slopes, so humans have tended to settle south-facing slopes first, building villages, clearing cropland, and planting orchards and vineyards.

them. Not an extensive collector himself, Engelmann became a collector of collections, and his personal herbarium formed the basis of the Missouri Botanical Garden Herbarium. **G, Y, T, R**

HUCKLEBERRIES

Traditional huckleberry grounds were as important as big-game hunting grounds to early Rocky Mountain peoples. Picking the juicy, bluish berries continues to be a seasonal highlight for some Native Americans and Anglos alike.

Huckleberries are in the *Vaccinium* genus, a tasty branch of the heath family. There are 15 species of *Vaccinium* in the Rockies and, depending on whom you ask, one or more of those species might be called huckleberry, blueberry, whortleberry, grouseberry, or bilberry. Two of the species commonly agreed to be huckleberry are *V. occidentale,* the western huckleberry, and *V. globulare,* the globe huckleberry.

These small- to medium-size shrubs are found in moist areas of the region, especially where soils have been disturbed by fire or logging. Look for them in clearings of lodgepole pine forests and other places with acid soil, from about 6,000 feet to 9,000 feet elevation.

The western huckleberry grows to about 2 feet tall, and the globe huckleberry shrub can be up to 6 feet tall. Globe huckleberry is most noticeable in the Rockies and produces the better berry harvest. Indigenous peoples gathered the ripe berries, typically 1/2 to 3/4 inch in diameter, and dried them in the sun for winter use. A tea was made from huckleberry roots and stems to treat rheumatism, heart trouble, and arthritis.

All Rocky Mountain *Vaccinium* species provide food for wildlife. Deer and elk eat the leaves; grouse, ptarmigan, coyotes, birds, rodents, and others eat the berries. Black and grizzly bears gorge on them, following ripening berries to higher elevations as late summer rolls into fall. In bad years, when berries are scarce, bears have been known to travel more than 100 miles between patches.

Today, huckleberries fuel a cottage industry of huckleberry syrup, jam, muffin mix, and the like. Look for cafe signs advertising huckleberry shakes.

G, Y, T, R

JUNIPERS

When is a berry not a berry? When it's a cone. Those little blue berries on the Rocky Mountain juniper are actually seed-bearing cones that take 2 years to ripen. At the end of the first summer, the new cones are green and very bitter. Check again at the end of the second summer, and you should find a frosty-looking, ripe, blue cone about the size of a pea. Look closely on the surface for 2 or more little points, equivalent to the sharp tips of pine cone scales.

Sometimes called cedar, Rocky Mountain juniper can be found

throughout the region on dry slopes and in canyons from about 5,000 to 8,000 feet. *Juniperus scopulorum* grows both as a shrub, to about 9 feet, and as a tree, to about 40 feet. In tree form, the juniper can have either a pointed or a rounded crown.

A juniper's foliage changes as the tree matures. Juvenile trees have sharp-pointed, awl-shaped needles, but when a plant is several years old, it begins to develop mature foliage of cedarlike scales, tightly pressed together. You might be able to make a comparison by finding juvenile foliage on shoots growing near the bottom of a mature juniper.

The other widespread juniper species in the Rockies, the common juniper (*J. communis*), grows strictly as a shrub and never develops the mature, scalelike foliage.

Juniper had important medicinal and spiritual applications in many Native American tribes. Some wafted the sacred smoke to purify the air and ward off disease. Others made a tea from the boughs, branches, and cones to treat colds, fevers, and pneumonia. Women drank juniper tea after giving birth for the purpose of cleansing and healing. Needles were burned as incense, sometimes to dispel a fear of thunder, and wood was used to make bows and spears. Cones were chewed to settle an upset stomach or stimulate the

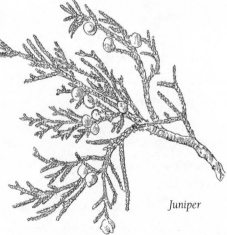

Juniper

• COOKING WITH JUNIPER BERRIES •

Juniper berries have too strong a flavor to eat, but they can add an exotic punch to potato salad and make a wonderful base for meat marinades.

In *Discovering Wild Plants*, author Janice Schofield recommends combining about 3 tablespoons of juniper berries (or a half-dozen berries per half-pound of meat) with 3/4 cup oil, 1/4 cup soy sauce, 1/4 cup vinegar, and 1/4 cup cooking wine. Marinate meat for about 24 hours and then roast, basting often.

In *Beard on Birds*, chef James Beard offers a recipe for sautéed quail with juniper berries in which he suggests browning quail in butter and seasoning with salt, pepper, and 1 to 2 tablespoons of chopped juniper berries. Cover, reduce heat, cook for 10 minutes, and don't forget to "pass the pan juices."

appetite. Cones and foliage also provide winter food and shelter for grouse and other birds as well as for deer and small mammals.

Some modern cookbooks offer recipes for meat sauce using juniper berries. And if you suddenly crave a gin and tonic as you prepare the sauce, you may recognize where gin gets its flavoring. **G, Y, T, R**

KINNIKINNICK

Kinnikinnick is probably the most common evergreen plant in the Rocky Mountain region. The spreading heath forms a dark green mat up to 6 inches thick over rocky soil in dry, open woods from the lowest elevations to the highest. Often considered an indicator of poor soil, kinnikinnick is, appropriately enough, a plant that builds soil and controls erosion.

You may recognize *Arctostaphylos uva-ursi* as the same ground cover used by commercial landscapers in plantings for roadways, parking strips, and other industrial habitats. The small, leathery, oval leaves grow on multibranched, woody stems with reddish, scaly bark. In May and early June, look for dainty, pink or white, urn-shaped flowers blooming in clusters at the ends of the branches. In late summer, flowers have given way to glossy red berries about the size of peas. Bears and other mammals and birds eat these berries through the winter, giving the plant its common name, bearberry. Bears are also referenced in the scientific name, which translates to "bear's grape." The twigs and leaves provide winter browse for deer, elk, and bighorn sheep.

Some indigenous peoples fried the berries or dried them for use as a condiment, but the mealy fruits weren't widely utilized for food. Leaves were the commodity on this plant. The word kinnikinnick derives from the Algonquian language and means "that which is mixed." Native Americans and early traders mixed kinnikinnick leaves with tobacco to create a

Kinnikinnick

milder smoking blend. In the absence of tobacco, kinnikinnick leaves were mixed with the dried inner bark of smooth-burning red-osier dogwood.

Lewis and Clark noticed that Canadian trading company clerks carried kinnikinnick leaves around with them in small bags. There may have been other reasons besides smoking for those clerks to be collecting leaves, as they contain tannic acid, which is useful in curing pelts. The leaves also contain gallic acid and several glycosides and were used medicinally to treat kidney and bladder ailments. **G, Y, T, R**

LIMBER PINE

Limber pines know how to shrug it off. Snow load and wind are no problem to this snow-country pine, whose flexible limbs can bend, sway, or whip without breaking. Look for *Pinus flexilis* scattered around the Rockies growing on exposed sites from the foothills to timberline.

The loose-limbed trees rarely exceed 50 feet, but they can have trunks up to a yard thick with dark, deeply furrowed bark. At extremely windy locations, limber pines grow gnarly and twisted, with the trunk sometimes separating into several branches.

Yellowish green needles are about 2 inches long and come in bundles of 5. The 3- to 6-inch-long cones are light brown and often pitchy, with slightly thickened, roundish-tipped scales.

Limber pines mature at about 300 years of age, and individuals in Idaho and Utah are known to have lived 1,300 or more years. Today, somewhere in the Rockies, there may be a limber pine that was a seedling when Buddha left home to begin his teachings.

Whitebark pine, a similar tree generally found at higher elevations, also has flexible limbs and 5-needle bundles. However, the cones of *P. albicaulis* are

• PINE, FIR, OR SPRUCE? •

First, look at the needles. Pine needles come in packets, fir are flat and friendly, and spruce have sides and are stickery. Not exactly scientific, but a reasonable rule of thumb in determining what kind of evergreen you're looking at.

Pine needles come in bundles of 2 to 5, packaged in thin, papery sheaths at the base. Spruce needles are sharp at the ends, grow singly, typically have 4 sides, and can be rolled between your thumb and finger like a pencil. Fir needles (including those of Douglas-fir, which isn't a true fir) also grow singly, but they're rounder on the ends and too flat to roll.

Next, consider the cones. Pine cones are sturdy and protective and commonly grow near the ends of branches. Ripe cones may remain on lodgepole and limber pines, but usually fall off the other species.

Spruce cones are papery, hang down from branches, and don't fall apart on the tree. The cones of true firs grow upright on the topmost branches and, when ripe, disintegrate in place instead of falling off the tree. Douglas-fir grows pendant cones with distinctive mouse-tail bracts; the cones drop off the tree when mature.

smaller, dark purple, and have thick, pointed scales. They also disintegrate on the tree at maturity, whereas the cones of limber pine stay intact on the tree. **G, Y, T, R**

LODGEPOLE PINE

Lodgepole pine is one of the most common coniferous trees in the Rockies. With its wide tolerance for conditions and habitat, the lodgepole can be found on 80 percent of the forested land in the region. Look for *Pinus contorta* in dry soil up to about 11,000 feet.

In the right conditions, trees can be 150 feet tall, but lodgepole is most conspicuous when it's growing in dense, almost claustrophobic stands, such as those found in Glacier and Yellowstone National Parks. In these "dog hair" thickets, trees grow slender and straight, and lower branches die off from lack of sunlight. Indians from the treeless Plains traveled great distances to harvest the straight-growing trees and sometimes traded for them to use as tipi lodgepoles. Women cut and peeled the poles, which were usually about 25 feet long and quite strong for their weight. Today, the larger lodgepole pines growing in more spacious stands are harvested to construct log houses, though power tools now peel the thin, scaly bark.

Stiff, 1- to 2-inch needles are yellowish and grow in bundles of 2. Roundish cones are only 1 to 2 inches long with thin, prickly scales, and are usually off-center at the base.

Lodgepole is considered a "fire species," since fire is an important component of the tree's life cycle. The tree has 2 types of cone, one of which opens to release seeds only when it's been heated to more than 130°F. Such high temperatures melt the resin that keeps the cones glued shut, keeping seeds viable for long periods of time and safe from hungry wildlife. These serotinous cones stay on the tree until a fire opens them, resulting in a massive postburn reseeding. New seedlings thrive in poor soil and full sun, so lodgepole forests may succeed themselves after a fire. They also usually succeed burned-out spruce and fir forests, because those evergreens need a little shade to grow well.

Appropriately enough, lodgepole forests are fires waiting to happen. They grow in dry conditions in dense stands, with dead lower branches and pitchy wood and bark. Most of the trees burned in the 1988 Yellowstone fire were lodgepole pine.

In between fires, lodgepole stands support a variety of wildlife, particularly bark-foraging birds such as woodpeckers and red squirrels, which exploit the nonserotinous cones that open as they dry. **G, Y, T, R**

PONDEROSA PINE

The ponderosa pine is the biggest and most widespread conifer in the region and—like some other confirmed westerners—won't be found much farther east than the Black Hills of South Dakota.

Under good growing conditions, the straight-trunked *Pinus ponderosa* grows up to 150 feet tall with a diameter of 2 to 5 feet. Branches are sparse, giving the tree a spare, open look. The stout needles are 8 to 10 inches long and grow in bundles of 3. Elliptical, reddish brown cones are 3 to 5 inches long. Mature trees have corky, orangish bark that grows in flat

Ponderosa Pines

THE GREAT ROCKY MOUNTAIN NATURE FACTBOOK

plates shaped something like big puzzle pieces. Put your nose to the bark and see if you can detect the scent of vanilla.

Unlike dense forests of Douglas-fir or lodgepole pine, ponderosa pines normally grow in stands of widely spaced trees that convey a parklike openness, even when you're standing among the trees. Needle litter and saplings provide good fuel for frequent ground fires, which keep the grassy understory free of brush. While saplings are vulnerable to fire, the thick bark and high crowns of mature trees make adult trees quite fire-resistant. If ground fires aren't allowed to burn, young ponderosa form a thicket among the larger trees.

Although Doug-fir is the commercial giant of North America, ponderosa pine is the most commercially valuable tree in the Rocky Mountain region. Most knotty pine paneling comes from young ponderosas, whereas the clear-grained, mature trees produce wood with pale sapwood and yellow to orangish brown heartwood.

Ponderosas are most common in the dry transition zone between grasslands and higher-elevation moist forests. That said, no other major western tree is more able to push its boundaries. "P-pines," as they're called locally, are drought-resistant and sun-tolerant as well as fire-resistant—all characteristics for success in the Rocky Mountain ecosystem. Drought resistance is the p-pine's tour de force. The tree's taproot may bore over 30 feet down into the soil and send root branches snaking out 100 feet in search of moisture. Needles are also capable of absorbing moisture to transfer

> **The thick bark and high crowns of mature ponderosa pine trees make adult trees quite fire-resistant.**

●

138

to roots, turning fog and dew into viable water sources.

The ponderosa's inner bark was an important food for indigenous peoples, a detail Sacajawea explained to Lewis and Clark. It was the women's job to strip bark and remove the sweet, edible layer. Before metal trade items were circulating, people made scrapers from the horns of mountain sheep. Later, women found that baking powder cans could be made into sharp tools perfect for the job.

Ponderosa pines provide food and shelter for a variety of wildlife too—from eagles, owls, and finches to squirrels, bats, and snakes. **T, R**

SAGEBRUSHES

If one picture is worth a thousand words, then one whiff of sagebrush is worth a thousand pictures. The character and history of the Rocky Mountain West live in that pungent scent, evocative of dry, wild openness.

There are many species of *Artemisia* living in a variety of arid to semiarid habitats from the foot of the Rocky Mountain Front to the peaks themselves. Most are highly aromatic, with shrubby, silvery foliage that blooms with tiny flowers in late summer. Birdsfoot sage (*A. pedatifida*) might grow only 2 inches tall, whereas big sagebrush (*A. tridentata*) can reach 8 feet.

Big sagebrush is one of the most abundant plants in the West, sometimes covering many square miles of dry, intermountain valley floor. The multibranched shrub has shaggy bark with no spines— not to be confused with the similar-looking, though spiny, greasewood, *Sarcobatus vermiculatus*, which grows only in saline soils. Big sage's small, soft, gray-green leaves are shaped something like long, 3-toed paws and persist on the plant over the winter, providing food for elk, mule deer, sage grouse, and pronghorns.

In the Lower 48, nearly 90 percent of the nation's public lands lie in the 11 western states. This means a third to a half of the land in each of those states is under federal management. East of the Rockies, states average about 2 percent to 5 percent public land.

Some federal land, such as military bases and bombing grounds, isn't open to the general public, but there is public access to a large portion of federally owned lands, including national forests, national parks, national wildlife refuges, and rangeland.

According to the extremely interesting and informative *Atlas of the New West: Portrait of a Changing Region,* the idea that the federal government should retain title to large landholdings first arose in the Congressional act that created Yellowstone National Park in 1872.

Yellowstone was managed by the U.S. Army until Congress created the National Park Service in 1916. By that time, Yosemite, Mesa Verde, and Grand Canyon National Parks had also been created. Congress also granted presidential authority to set aside and manage forest reserves, and, between Presidents Harrison and Cleveland, about 40 million acres were designated as national forest. Poring over maps one March night in 1907, President Teddy Roosevelt and Gifford Pinchot, first head of the Forest Service, designated 16 million additional acres of forestland in 33 separate proclamations—beating a proposed Congressional act rescinding presidential authority to withdraw land from homesteading. Two of the "midnight forests" were Cascade National Forest in Washington and Oregon, and Grand Mesa in Colorado.

The vast open ranges were the next lands to be placed under federal authority. In 1934, the Grazing Service, which would become the Bureau of Land Management (BLM), was given the responsibility of regulating grazing and mineral leases on nearly 150 million acres of land that had belonged to the federal government since the Louisiana Purchase but had never been claimed under the Homestead Act.

Each public-lands agency has a separate mandate, sometimes putting it in conflict with a sister agency. As the *Atlas of the New West* points out, public lands have become a battlefield between the "Old West" (whose interests include grazing, timber and resource extraction, and the preservation of traditional lifestyles) and the "New West" (with its sometimes conflicting desires for wildland recreation and wilderness preservation).

Indian reservations are sovereign lands, outside the control of federal or state government.

The various sage species were used widely by indigenous peoples in medicinal and ceremonial ways. According to *Montana Native Plants and Early Peoples,* prairie sage, *A. ludoviciana,* was considered "man sage" by Cheyenne Indians and was probably included in more religious ceremonies than any other plant, often for purification.

Fringed sage, *A. frigida,* was considered "woman sage" and used in a tea to regulate menstruation. Tea was also made from big sagebrush to treat colds and pneumonia. In addition, big sage was used for firewood since it was plentiful, smelled good, and even live plants readily burned.

Peterson's *Rocky Mountain Wildflowers* notes that the first white people to arrive in western valleys found sagebrush and grass growing together, though grass seemed to dominate, keeping the spread of sage in check. In many areas of the West, overgrazing by domestic livestock has gradually weakened the grasses, and since livestock doesn't readily eat sagebrush, grasslands have become sagebrush lands. This is a good-news, bad-news situation. The bad news is that intact, native grass ecosystems are nearly gone from the West. The good news is that sagebrush provides food and shelter for a variety of wildlife species, especially in the winter, when it is most needed. Sagebrush is high in fat, and although most animals can't subsist only on the strong leaves, the plant makes a good supplemental food source. Small animals find it a welcome and secure place in which to den, nest, and otherwise take shelter.

Plants in the *Artemisia* genus are more closely related to tarragon than to the cooking herb we call sage, which is actually in the mint family. **G, Y, T, R**

SERVICEBERRY

Serviceberry celebrates the Rocky Mountain spring by strewing white flower-petal

Before there were Power Bars, there was pemmican. This calorie-dense food was developed by Native Americans and adopted by Northwest trappers, traders, and mountain men. A little bit goes a long way, and if stored in a cool, dry place, pemmican will keep for months.

Buffalo was the original base meat, but pemmican can be made with venison, elk, moose, or beef. Serviceberry was the most popular fruit for pemmican, though currants, gooseberries, hawthorn berries, and chokecherries were also used.

To make pemmican, cut meat into strips and dry completely, either in the sun or in an oven. In the oven, cook meat strips at low heat (about 250°F) for 4 to 6 hours, or until thoroughly dry. Grind or pound the dried meat to an almost powderlike consistency and mix it with an equal amount of melted animal fat. Suet may be used. Add fresh or dried berries to fortify the mixture, and salt to taste. Knead the ingredients into a paste and pack in sausage casings or cheesecloth.

Pemmican can be eaten with no further preparation, or it can be boiled into a porridge or fried like sausage.

confetti across the greening land. The most common, early-blooming shrub of the northern Rockies, serviceberry can hold its small but profuse blossoms for as long as a month after flowers begin to open around the first week of May. The thick fragrance, mixed with the unlocking aromas of spring soil, is restorative.

Keep your eyes and nose alert for the 3- to 20-foot, thornless *Amelanchier alnifolia* growing on moist ground near streams and creeks and in the mountains to about 7,500 feet. The toothed, roundish leaves are 1 to 2 inches long and turn red or yellow in the fall before dropping off.

The 1/4- to 1/2-inch serviceberry fruits were one of the most important berry crops for indigenous peoples. More closely related to an apple than a berry, the dark blue to purple pomes have 2 to 3 seeds surrounded by flesh that can be quite juicy and sweet. Along with chokecherries, serviceberries were a common ingredient in pemmican (a traditional food made of meat, fat, and berries).

Pounded and whole fruits were dried and formed into cakes for preservation. Lewis and Clark noted that these serviceberry patties could weigh up to 15 pounds. The dried fruit was used in meat stews, or mixed with sugar, flour, and water to make a pudding. In addition to food, larger shrubs produced strong but flexible wood for arrow shafts and tipi stakes.

Also called saskatoonberry and juneberry, the fruit generally ripens in

Serviceberry

July and is still gathered and used in pancakes and muffins, or made into jam, pie, and wine.

Given a choice, browsers such as deer, elk, moose, mountain goats, bighorn sheep, rodents, and rabbits will all select this shrub over anything else. Grouse, bears, coyotes, and other species stuff themselves with the fruits. In the fall, look for serviceberry seeds in animal scat.

Serviceberry is most likely to be confused with chokecherry, although the latter is generally larger and more treelike. Both plants are early bloomers but, typically, serviceberry blooms first. Also, chokecherries have one pit instead of the several seeds found in a serviceberry. **G, Y, T, R** (See Chokecherry)

SNOWBERRIES

Just so a person doesn't get too lonesome for snow during the summer, there's snowberry. This abundant shrub, a member of the honeysuckle family, grows throughout the Rocky Mountain region.

Mountain snowberry is a 1- to 3-foot, multibranched plant with oval leaves and small, pink, funnel-shaped flowers. Look for *Symphoricarpos oreophilus* on slopes and in ravines of the montane zone. A second species of snowberry, also called buckbrush (*S. albus*), grows from low-elevation valleys into the subalpine zone. The two look quite similar except the flowers of buckbrush are bell-shaped. In late summer, both species produce large, white berries up to 1/2 inch in diameter.

Snowberries have never been an important food source for people, but they are eaten by birds and other animals. The *Cascade-Olympic Natural History Trailside Reference* reports that an Indian name for this berry translates as "good for the kids to throw at each other."

Although snowberry bushes didn't provide food, the plant did have medicinal application. Several tribes used the crushed leaves, berries, and bark in poultices to encourage healing and reduce scarring. Some Native American tribes tell a funny story about how Coyote made arrows from the shrub's crooked branches. **G, Y, T, R**

SUBALPINE FIR

This isn't the biggest, longest-lived, or widest-ranging tree around, but its symmetrical beauty and alluring fragrance make this fir a special presence in the Rockies. It was believed that bad spirits, nightmares, and ghosts could be warded off by hanging fir branches on the walls of Native American lodges. After a death, smoke from burning fir was used to purify the dwelling. The tree's needles were pounded for use as hair tonic, perfume, and baby powder. Tea made from the resin and needles was used for coughs and colds, and fir boughs were burned in sweat lodges to purify and scent the air.

The term "krummholz" comes from the German *krumm*, meaning "crooked," and *holz*, meaning "wood," and refers to the stunted, gnarled, and sometimes matlike growth of trees at high elevations. Snow insulates the trees near ground level, protecting them from frigid winds that kill off any branches outside the snow's protection. Summer winds also contribute to the shaping of krummholz by inhibiting growth on the windward side of the plant.

Flag trees, also shaped by high-elevation winds, have the look of blowing flags or banners, even in still air. The good news is that those dead windward branches help protect the rest of the tree. Unlike the low-growing, matlike "cushion" form of some plants, krummholz and flagging are functions of environment. If you take the seeds from such gnarled trees and plant them in a less harsh setting, normal trees will grow. Subalpine fir, Engelmann spruce, limber pine, and whitebark pine can all be found growing as krummholz and flag trees. (See Moss Campion)

Also called alpine fir, balsam fir, and white balsam, *Abies lasiocarpa* grows in moist, high-elevation habitats up to the tree line throughout the region. Reaching heights of 40 to 100 feet, the subalpine fir develops a slender, spirelike crown and has shortish, symmetrical, horizontal branches perfect for hanging Christmas ornaments on. The flat needles are about an inch long and curve up from the stem on J-shaped bases, as opposed to growing straight out from the stem. Cones are purple, about 3 inches long, and grow pointing upward. On young trees, the light gray bark is smooth and thin, but bark thickens and roughens as the tree matures. Look for resin blisters or pockets on the bark. Like other true firs, subalpine firs develop extensive resin blisters, possibly explaining why the tree gives off such a strong fragrance. Also look for drooping lower branches. Subalpine fir reproduces by layering, where branches that touch the soil take root.

At timberline, the tree may be stunted into a prostrate form called krummholz. Subalpine fir is also a common "flag tree," meaning branches grow only on the lee side of the trunk. At high elevations, notice where harsh winds have created windrows of subalpine fir. **G, Y, T, R**

SYRINGA

By the time Captain Meriwether Lewis "discovered" *Philadelphus lewisii,* Native Americans had long been using its wood for arrow shafts. Also known as Indian arrow-wood and mock orange, the 3- to 10-foot, multibranched shrub looks something like a dogwood and can bloom in such profusion that it covers hillsides like a floral quilt. Flowers are about 1 1/2 inches across, with 4 white

petals fringed in the center with yellow stamens. Look for syringa in western Montana and Idaho (where it's the state flower), blooming from the latter part of May through July on medium-dry to moist ground along streams, on hillsides, and in the mountains to about 7,000 feet.

Syringa, which is in the hydrangea family, often grows in the company of serviceberry, chokecherry, and Rocky Mountain maple. Although those other woody plants are favorite foods of deer, syringa is not. Wildlife managers look to the shrub for an indication of how many deer are browsing a winter range. If deer are eating the syringa, use is considered heavy. But just to keep wildlife managers on their toes, deer and elk in some localized spots seem to show a decided preference for the shrub.

The fragrant, beautiful, deer-resistant shrub can be cultivated and is used extensively in landscape plantings. **G**

ARROWLEAF BALSAMROOT

Arrowleaf balsamroot sweeps over dry hillsides like a yellow tide. Known in some areas as sunflower, the 2- to 3-inch, yellow flower blooms in early spring and can be up to 2 feet tall. Foot-long, arrow-shaped leaves covered with silvery-gray fuzz grow from near the base.

Look for large patches of *Balsamorhiza sagittata* in dry valleys and foothills and in the mountains to about 8,000 feet.

Some Native peoples peeled the immature flower stems and ate the inner portion like celery. Flathead Indians made use of the woody roots, baking them in fire pits for at least 3 days,

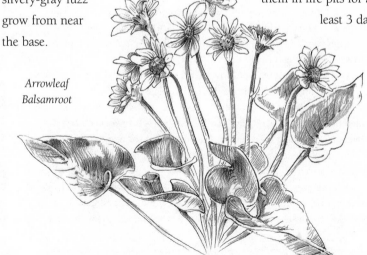

Arrowleaf Balsamroot

• SPLENDOR OF THE GRASS •

A field of grasses bending in a Rocky Mountain wind can be as beautiful as any meadow of wildflowers—especially if you know its importance to the ecosystem. Grasses, which grow in all climates, cover more than one-fifth of the earth's land surface. These precious plants prevent erosion by drawing moisture from rainwater and snowmelt into the earth and holding soil in place with their roots. And as grasses die and regenerate, a huge amount of valuable organic material is added to the soil. Many species of wild and domestic animals rely heavily on grasses for food—from large grazing animals to seed-eating birds to rodents. Humans also depend on such grasses as wheat, oats, corn, barley, and rice.

Whereas wildflowers are classified by families, grasses are further classified into tribes, including the fescue tribe (to which the bluegrasses and bromegrasses belong) and the gramma, oat, timothy, and wheat tribes.

Within the tribes are 2 basic types of grasses: sod formers and bunchgrasses. Sod formers spread their stems horizontally, sending leaves up and roots down to form a continuous, interwoven mat of sod. For instance, buffalo grass *(Buchloë dactyloides)*, a native short grass of the Rocky Mountain region's high plains and low foothills, grows to about 4 inches tall and forms a dense, tough sod.

Bunchgrasses grow in tufts, never forming a tight sod. Sheep fescue *(Festuca ovina)* is a native bunchgrass found to 11,000 feet, with fine, short leaves growing up to a foot tall. The fescues are among the most important grasses for grazing animals.

A moderate amount of grazing can actually be healthful to a range, as grassland is improved by the growth of new grass. But there is a direct relationship between leaf growth and root growth. If the grass in an area is eaten more than halfway down, the root system is overwhelmed and the plant suffers, leading over time to degeneration of soil and grasses. However, if grass plants are grazed no more than halfway down overall, the range will remain vigorous.

Unfortunately, little in the way of western land use has been moderate. With grazing, agriculture, road building, and suburban development, large, unbroken expanses of lower-elevation native grasslands no longer exist.

like camas. Nez Percé people roasted and ground the seeds, which they mixed with animal fat and rolled into little balls.

The leaves could be used in poultices for burns, and root poultices were applied to treat cuts and bruises.

Elk and deer graze shoots, and bighorn sheep favor the leaves and flowers. Horses also eat the flowers. Sturdy plant that it is, arrowleaf balsamroot can withstand heavy grazing. **G, Y, T**

BITTERROOT

The cover of Peterson's *Rocky Mountain Wildflowers* field guide features a lovely pink bitterroot bloom growing on a dark gray rock. It's a fitting choice, given this plant's beauty and significance to the region.

Lewisia rediviva grows in rocky, dry soil of valleys, foothills, mountain slopes, and high ridges of the region to about 8,000 feet.

Bitterroot's many-petaled pink to whitish flower is about

2 inches across and rests atop a 1- to 3-inch stem. A long, slender bud is often present with the open flower. Before the plant is in bloom, look for small tufts of 1- to 2-inch-long, fat, fingerlike leaves growing from a thick crown. The leaves sprout in late winter under the snow or even on bare ground. By the time the flower appears (late April into July), the leaves have withered nearly completely away, making bitterroot appear leafless.

Bitterroot's thick, starchy root was a staple food for indigenous peoples. The raw root was truly bitter, though most of the unpleasantness could be boiled out. Women dug the root with special tools before the plant bloomed, identifying it by the leaf tufts. Ceremonies involving elder women often marked the digging of the season's first root.

An elder woman is featured in a Flathead story of how bitterroot came to be. It seems as though, a long time ago in what is now the

Bitterroot Valley of Montana, people were starving. One old woman, who had no food to feed her sons, went down to the river to weep and sing a death song. The rising sun heard her weeping and sent a guardian spirit in the form of a rose-colored bird. The bird told the woman that a plant would be created from her tears, which had fallen into the soil, from the white of her hair, and from the red of the bird. The bird said that when people saw the flower they would know that a mother's tears had given them food.

Rediviva does mean "brought to life," although it doesn't refer to this story. Lewis and Clark sent a root back East, and after 3,000 circuitous miles, a gardener at the Academy of Natural Science in Philadelphia was able to get the plant to sprout. **Y, T**

CAMAS

Camas once grew so plentifully in the western states that travelers occasionally mistook camas meadows for lakes. Although not as abundant as it once was, camas still grows along stream banks and in meadows, especially on the west side of the continental divide.

The camas's purplish blue flowers grow in a spiky cluster atop the 1- to 2-foot-tall plant. The underground bulb of *Camassia quamash,* a member of the lily family, was once among the most important food and trade items in the region. In *Montana Native Plants and Early Peoples,* author and ethnobotanist Jeff Hart explains that "Due to differences in quality and abundance, camas constituted an item of considerable trade among various Indian groups. Thus, Shoshoni traded it to Nez Percé; Nez Percé traded it to Gros Ventre and Crow; Upper Pend d'Oreille traded it to Kootenai; Kootenai traded it to Blackfeet, and so on. One reason why Flatheads traded for it with Nez Percé, for instance, was that they

• THE ORIGINAL PIT BARBECUE •

The earth-oven system of cooking roots, especially camas, was common to most Native American tribes in the Rocky Mountain region. Using digging sticks, flat rocks, and wide pieces of wood, pits were excavated near traditional gathering grounds and used from year to year.

Early pits were circular, though rectangular pits came into use later, apparently after European contact. Pits varied in size depending on the volume of roots to be cooked, though they could be 6 to 10 feet across and 2 to 3 feet deep. Women placed softball-size stones around, under, on top of, or among firewood laid in the pit, and after the stones had become hot enough, they were covered with earth and such plants as alder, arrowleaf balsamroot, willow, and skunk cabbage. Camas bulbs were placed on top of the vegetation, which had been wetted down to prevent the camas from burning. A layer of bark was added, and then the whole thing was covered with more dirt; a hole or hollow tube was often poked into the oven to let steam escape or to allow water to be poured in to prevent the camas from burning.

To maintain heat, a fire was built on top and maintained for 12 to 70 hours, again depending on the volume of roots being cooked. Bulbs were judged done either by the aroma coming from the pit or by digging some up and checking to see if they had turned dark brown or black, indicating they were completely baked.

Proficiency in cooking camas was a mark of distinction among Native American women since the process required a great deal of experience, patience, and care. Men assisted in gathering firewood, though it was customary for them to stay away from the ovens while the bulbs were cooking.

preferred its larger size and superior flavor to their own."

Women dug bulbs with digging sticks made of elk antlers or fire-hardened wood, plunging the stick into the ground next to the plant and rocking the digger back and forth until the soil was loose enough to reach in and take the bulb. Bulbs were usually roasted in underground ovens. Some bulbs were eaten immediately;

others were dried and stored for later use. Early Jesuit missionary Father Pierre-Jean De Smet described cooked camas as having the consistency of a jujube.

Before whites brought sugar into the territory, camas was the prime source of sweetener. The word *camas* can be traced back to a Nootka Indian word for "sweet." Unlike most other bulbs and rootstocks used for food, camas contains no starch. It's mostly composed of a sugar that breaks down into digestible fructose during the cooking process.

The Kootenai Indians tell a story about the time Coyote went to visit Moose. In the spirit of generosity, Moose "slapped his backsides and camas came out." In fact, cooked camas bulbs look something like moose droppings.

A plant called death camas (*Zigadenus venenosus*) grows in the same habitat as camas and has a similar-looking bulb. White camas, as it's also called, contains alkaloids that are toxic to humans and animals. When in bloom, the 2 plants are easily told apart by death camas's creamy white flowers. **G, Y, T**

COLUMBINE

Many plants in the Rocky Mountains have medicinal value and are able to soothe various ailments through their

Columbine

bitter teas. Columbine makes you feel good just by looking at it.

The 1- to 3-inch flowers of the Colorado blue columbine, *Aquilegia coerulea,* have 5 white petal-like sepals set within 5 outer petals that range in color from light to deep blue. Each blue outer petal has a long spur off the back. *Aquilegia* comes from the Latin for "eagle," a reference to the flower's talonlike spurs. *Coerulea* means "blue." High-elevation plants are generally deeper blue than those found at lower elevations. The color also becomes less pronounced north or west of Colorado, where Colorado blue columbine is the state flower.

Softly lobed compound leaves are clustered mostly around the base of the blue columbine, which can reach 3 feet tall. Look for this elegant member of the buttercup family in a wide variety of Rocky Mountain habitats, from the moist soil of aspen groves to exposed rock slides and outcrops, from

about 6,000 feet to 11,000 feet. The plant may cover a large area at higher elevations, a sight as sure to take away your breath as the thin, mountain air.

The talonlike spurs are filled with nectar, drawing hummingbirds and insects with long-enough tongues. Less-endowed insects have been known to bite through the knobs on the ends of the spurs to get a sweet drink.

There are other columbines in the Rockies, in addition to the Colorado blue. The yellow columbine grows in montane and subalpine woods and is common in Yellowstone and Glacier National Parks; flowers of *A. flavescens* can be pale yellow to salmon-colored. **G, Y, T, R**

FAIRY SLIPPER ORCHID

A glimpse of fairy slipper orchids in the deep, quiet forest is enough to make some sensitive souls feel they've slipped through to the Middle Kingdom.

The delicate flowers bloom briefly from late May until late June, soon after snow melts and before too many wanderers are in the woods. Look for a single, purplish pink flower atop a straight, slender stem about 2½ to 5 inches tall.

The flower's elongated lower petal is cupped just so, waiting to receive a fairy's slender foot. The single, large, oval leaf that grows at the base of the stem unfurls in late summer or fall, persists through the winter, and withers soon after the flower blooms in the spring.

Fairy slippers, or Calypso orchids (Calypso bulbosa), grow throughout the Rockies in the shade of moist, evergreen woods from about 5,000 to 8,000 feet. The shadowy beauty was named after Calypso, the sea nymph of Homer's Odyssey, who waylaid the homeward-bound Odysseus for 7 years.

Orchidaceae is one of the largest plant families. Most of the 20,000 species are tropical, but there are about 30 orchids in the Rockies. The majority have small, inconspicuous flowers, but still exhibit the distinctive, pouty lower "lip."

Orchids have a special relationship with soil fungi; in fact, some species can germinate only when the appropriate fungus is present. This is one reason orchids are difficult to cultivate. Fungal threads called hyphae penetrate into the orchid and pump in water and nutrients. Perhaps as an evolutionary result of this relationship, most orchids have shallow, poorly developed roots. The Calypso orchid's underground corm, or bulblike, fleshy stem, is so shallow that any disturbance might damage or destroy the plant.

Overenthusiastic flora collectors have contributed to the demise of some orchid species. The Rocky Mountain yellow lady's slipper (Cypripedium calceolus) is now an endangered species. **G, Y, T, R**

The moist forests of the Rocky Mountains bulge with fungi in spring and fall, especially in areas that have been touched by wildfire.

Neither plant nor animal, fungi are in their own eponymous kingdom. Mushrooms, including the region's highly edible morel, are the fruiting bodies of fungi, although not all species produce mushrooms. The wispy snow mold seen covering the ground when snow melts away is an example of a nonfruiting fungus.

Fungi reproduce by releasing spores, which produce threadlike growths called hyphae. The hyphae grow and fuse with other hyphae into bundles called mycelia, from which mushrooms may sprout. Mycelia can live for centuries, producing generation after generation of mushrooms. Chances are, any shovelful of dirt you turn over in a Rocky Mountain forest, woodland, or grassland will contain hyphae.

Like animals, fungi don't produce their own food. Since they can't graze or hunt, mushrooms can be parasitic or saprophytic (obtaining nutrients from already decaying wood and plant matter) or can combine with photosynthetic algae to form a lichen co-op in which fungi provide the structure while algae provide the food.

The fourth fungal approach to food gathering may change the way you perceive the natural world. Mycorrhizal fungi have developed symbiotic relationships between their hyphae and certain plant species, such as the fairy slipper orchid. In fact, more than 90 percent of trees and green plants are vitally connected to mycorrhizal fungi, which include chanterelles and truffles. Fungal filaments wrap roots like so many cobwebs, essentially increasing the surface area of the root and acting like extra root hairs.

In exchange for photosynthetically produced carbohydrates, mycorrhizae provide their associate plants with minerals, nitrogen, and water. Mycorrhizally assisted water exchange is so efficient that conifers with such relationships are twice as drought-resistant as nonassociated trees. Citrus trees require less fertilizer when grown with mycorrhizae. Since it is in their interest to protect their associates, mycorrhizal fungi release chemicals that fight certain disease microorganisms present in the soil.

Because mycorrhizal hyphae form extensive networks through the soil from plant to plant, some researchers believe that resources may be shared among individual plants. For example, seedlings might receive nutrients from stronger plants, and water from deep-rooted trees may be shared with shallow-rooted neighbors during dry spells.

GLACIER LILY

When the blankets of snow are finally thrown off, glacier lilies are among the first to rise and greet the spring sun. Found throughout the region, *Erythronium grandiflorum* appears at low elevations in early April and then follows the receding snow line, blooming later at elevations up to 12,000 feet. The 6- to 15-inch-tall flowers are daffodil yellow, with pointed petals curled back from the slender, nodding stem. Actually, the petals and sepals are indistinguishable, so those yellow parts are correctly known as tepals. One to 3 flowers grow from a single bulb.

Look for this member of the lily family growing in patches in a variety of Rocky Mountain habitats, including sagebrush slopes, stream banks, moist meadows, and shady woods. Also known as dogtooth violet, snow lily, and fawn lily, the plant has bulbs that are edible but that were apparently never used extensively for food by indigenous peoples. The fresh, green seed pods are said to taste like string beans when boiled, and are enjoyed raw by elk, deer, and bighorn sheep.

Grizzly and black bears dig and eat the bulbs, which are also harvested for winter food by some small rodents. **G, Y, T, R**

LUPINE

At least a dozen lupine species—including silvery, silky, short-stemmed, low, velvet, and cushion—can be found scattered in the Rocky Mountains from valley bottom to mountaintop. Depending on the species and habitat, this member of the pea family grows from 2 inches to over 2 feet tall. Flowers are purple to blue or white, clustered on elongated racemes. Below the flower are 5- to 9-fingered leaves that look like a fan or palm frond. After a summer rain, single drops of water may lie like crystal beads in the lupine's satiny palm. Watch for blooming "bluebonnets" or "quakerbonnets" from June into the first part of August.

The genus name, *Lupinus,* comes from *lupus,* for "wolf." At one time it was thought that lupines stole nutrients from the soil, but we have learned that the tiny bacteria living in the "wolfbean" actually fix nitrogen, benefiting the soil.

As the seed pods of some species ripen, they concentrate bitter alkaloids that can be toxic to livestock—although the plant becomes safe for consumption again after the seeds are ripe. Wild animals either know when to eat lupine or are unaffected by the toxins: black and grizzly bears eat seeds, pods, and roots; elk and deer browse flowers and seed pods; and mice feed on roots and seeds. **G, Y, T, R**

Lupine

MINTS

I f you find yourself thinking about mint juleps while scrambling down a wet stream bank, there's a reason. You've probably just stepped on *Mentha arvensis* and are getting a good waft of minty aroma. Also known as field mint, this native plant was well known to indigenous Rocky Mountain peoples for its medicinal properties. Mint

• LEGUMES: LUPINES TO LENTILS •

There are about 17,000 species of legumes—nitrogen-fixing plants from lupines to lentils to sweet peas, most of which bear their seeds in a pod. Small nodules on the roots contain nitrogen-fixing bacteria, which supply this essential nutrient to the plant. Whereas most plants must take their nitrogen directly from the soil, the legume's nodules allow it to thrive in nitrogen-poor soils.

Under favorable conditions, root nodule bacteria fix so much nitrogen that excess nitrogen is secreted into the soil. This is why domestic legume crops, such as soybeans and alfalfa, are sometimes rotated with nonlegumes such as corn and wheat. After the soybeans are harvested or alfalfa is cut, roots left in the ground are turned under to decompose and further boost soil nitrogen levels.

Nitrogen is essential to the formation of protein, so with their reliable source of nitrogen, leguminous plants are high in protein.

tea was drunk to treat colds, coughs, headaches, and kidney complaints. Leaves were packed around aching teeth to bring relief, and poultices were also used to ease rheumatism and arthritis. Wild mint leaves were also reportedly hung in lodges for the pleasant smell and were sprinkled on meat and berries to repel insects.

Look for this aromatic, 1- to 3-foot-tall perennial blooming in July, August, and early September along streams and in bogs and wet woods to about 9,000 feet. Light blue to pink flowers grow in the crotch, where the fine-toothed leaf meets the square stem. Before you crush a leaf to inhale the wonderful fragrance, be sure you have identified the plant correctly. Field mint resembles stinging nettle, which grows in the same moist habitats and also has a square stem and toothed leaves, and whose tiny prickers will leave you with a nasty sting, as the name implies.

Mints secrete oils that are volatile enough to evaporate without leaving a stain on paper or fabric. Menthol is distilled from a variety of *M. arvensis*.

Two other mints are native to the Rockies. Horsemint (*Monarda fistulosa*), also known as beebalm, lemon mint, and wild bergamot, grows in medium-dry to moist soil up to about 7,000 feet. This plant can also be used to make tea. Giant hyssop (*Agastache urticifolia*) grows in the moist soil of foothills. It wasn't commonly used for teas, although Native Americans reportedly ate the seeds. **G, Y, T, R**

MOSS CAMPION

Alpine plants have "learned" that one good way to survive harsh mountain climates is to hunker down. Moss campion learned the lesson beautifully and is widely distributed above timberline across the meadows, talus slopes, and exposed ridges of the high Rockies from about 9,000 to 12,000 feet.

Silene acaulis forms a mossy, cushionlike mat covered with small pink flowers that bloom from early July to mid-August. Mats are a multitude of narrow leaves measuring 3/8 inch to 3/4 inch in size and are typically about an inch high and a foot or more across. Keeping their heads all the way down, the 1/4-inch, 5-petaled flowers grow directly on the mat; *acaulis* means "stemless."

This species is found at northern latitudes around the earth, growing at sea level in the Arctic and at progressively higher elevations the farther south it's found. Moss campion is in the pink family, a reference not to the fact that the flower is pink, but that it's notched, or "pinked" (as in pinking shears), at the tip.

Phlox is another common alpine cushion plant, but phlox can be distinguished by a little well formed in the center of the flower or by its unnotched petals.

The term "cushion plant" is generic, referring to many different

Plant identification can be intimidating to the beginning botanist. But take heart: with only a little practice, it's fairly easy to distinguish at least the various flower families—an important first step. A good field guide can help you become familiar with the most common groups. Descriptions of some of the more familiar Rocky Mountain families follow.

Figwort (Scrophulaceae): This showy family includes paintbrush, penstemon, monkey flower, and butter-and-eggs. Figwort flowers have 2 liplike petals that are usually lobed.

Legume (Leguminosae): The irregular flowers of this family are often described as butterflylike. They have 5 petals: an upper banner petal, 2 wing petals, and 2 lower petals folded in a keel shape. Legumes have pea- or beanlike seed pods and include lupine, clover, milkvetch, locoweed, and wild licorice.

Lily (Liliaceae): Lilies are often showy, with 3 sepals and 3 petals that may look so alike they appear as 6 petals. The leaves are grasslike and have parallel veins. Roots are usually in the form of bulbs or corms. Wild onion, camas, glacier lily, yucca, and beargrass are all in the Lily family.

Orchid (Orchidaceae): This is one of the world's largest families of flowering plants. Most species are found in the tropics, although there are about 30 species in the Rockies. Most in this region have small, inconspicuous flowers, but the flowers nevertheless display the distinctive orchid characteristic of a pouty lower lip. Fairy slipper, coral root, and rattlesnake plantain are examples of regional orchids.

Phlox (Polemoniaceae): The flowers of this family are quite similar, with a saucer-shaped flower of 5 fused petals resting atop a funnel-shaped tube. Phloxes include sky pilot, Jacob's ladder, and alpine phlox.

Rose (Rosaceae): Cup-shaped flowers of the rose family have 5 separated petals. Rose species can be herbaceous plants, shrubs, or trees. Members include wild rose, wild strawberry, chokecherry, and mountain ash.

Sunflower (Asteraceae): Formerly referred to as the Compositae family, this is the largest family of seed-bearing plants, with over 500 species in the Rocky Mountains alone. There is great variety in the group, though all have very small flowers crowded onto a compact head, creating the effect of a single flower. Flowers may be arranged in rays around the head, such as in daisies, or tiny, tubular flowers may form a disklike head, such as in the dandelion.

plants that grow in a spreading, prostrate form. Cushion plants are among the first to colonize gravelly, barren high ground. Although they keep a low profile, the mats send out long taproots to anchor themselves against fierce mountain winds. Above ground, thick mats of dense shoots trap heat and moisture. The mats also tend to catch soil particles and old, decomposing leaves so that eventually the mats provide a fertile foothold for other high-country plants.

Although cushion growth form is an adaptation to the environment, it is perpetuated by genetics. If you cultivate moss campion away from wind and harsh weather, it will still grow as a mat, a feature that hasn't escaped the notice of rock gardeners.

A wide variety of plant families in addition to the phlox and pink families have evolved cushion species. This is an example of convergent evolution, in which plants sharing similar environments evolved similar-looking species.

Cushion plants are well equipped to meet the natural challenges of alpine life—which didn't include hordes of hikers until the last seconds of earth time. Research has shown that it may take 20 years for a cushion plant community to recover from a single summer of human foot traffic. **G, Y, T, R**

PAINTBRUSH

One could hardly paint a Rocky Mountain landscape without brushes. The region's pastoral scenes are colored by 24 different paintbrushes, all in the genus *Castilleja*. Most are either red or yellow, but hybridization is common, and these flowers that appear to have been dipped in paint also come in shades of pink, orange, and white.

Look for major showings of the brilliant red Wyoming paintbrush (*C. linariaefolia*) in June, July, and the first part of August in dry to moist soils from low-elevation valleys up to 9,000 feet. This species, which shares the nickname "Indian paintbrush" with several others, is Wyoming's state flower.

On close observation, you'll see that the color in this 1- to 3-foot-tall plant doesn't come from the flowers themselves, but from specialized leaves. These brightly colored leaves partially

Paintbrush

enclose the yellowish green, tubular flowers that grow in clusters at the top of the plant. Hummingbirds, bees, and butterflies are drawn to this nectar-producing beauty from the figwort family.

Like many of the other species, Wyoming paintbrush is semi-parasitic, making only a portion of its own food supply. Paintbrush sends out roots until they come into contact with the roots of a neighboring plant, often sagebrush. The paintbrush root penetrates the other to embezzle food. Over biological time, this relationship has become so established that *Castilleja* can scarcely survive without it. This is one reason paintbrushes are hard to cultivate domestically. **G, Y, T, R**

PASQUE FLOWER

These gorgeous lavender goblets usually arrive in time for Easter. The name of the pasque flower is derived from the Middle English word *Pasch,* meaning Easter or Passover, which is around the time the flowers bloom. The delicate cups may be 1 to 1½ inches across on stems 2 to 12 inches tall. Leaves are frilly. The entire plant, including the flower, is covered with fine hairs that trap heat and moisture and give the plant a soft, fuzzy look.

Pasque Flower

A member of the buttercup family, *Anemone patens* may grow singly or in clumps. Also called blue tulip or wild crocus, pasque flowers can be seen as early as March at lower elevations in moist but well-drained meadows, fields, and woods east of the continental divide. At higher elevations (they're found up to 9,000 feet), you may find them blooming in June.

The showy pasque flower actually has no petals. Those Easter-egg-pastel, petal-like things are modified leaves called sepals. When the sepals turn brown and fall off, the stem continues to grow, and the flower head becomes a tuft of long, feathery plumes. In this incarnation the plant is sometimes called prairie smoke, but that name actually belongs to the long-plumed avens, *Geum triflorum*. **G, Y, T, R**

PRICKLY PEAR CACTUS

Cacti aren't the first things that come to mind when thinking about the Rockies, but there is one common and fairly widespread representative. Your dog is sure to find prickly pear should you let her out to run in some of the region's arid zones. *Opuntia polyacantha* grows in dry

• FLOWERS: STEM TO STAMEN •

Flowers house the reproductive organs of flowering plants; the four main parts of a flower are the sepals, petals, stamens, and pistil.

Sepals enclose and protect the flower bud before it blooms. They are usually green and look more like leaves than petals, but notable exceptions include the showy, colored sepals of the pasque flower and Rocky Mountain iris.

Petals, often brightly colored, serve as advertisement and stage for bees, butterflies, and other pollinators.

Stamens are the flower's male part. At the tip of each stamen is an anther, in which pollen develops.

The pistil houses the flower's female parts, which are called stigma, style, and ovary. At the top of the pistil, the stigma receives pollen, which moves down the style, or pollen tube, to ovules in the ovary. Fertilization occurs in the ovule, which develops into a seed. While the seed is developing, the ovary matures into a fruit, which protects the seed and facilitates its dispersal.

Flowers are grouped into different types of inflorescences, which also help identify plant species. Some plants, such as sagebrush, grow flower spikes, in which individual flowers with little or no stems grow along a stalk. In racemes, flowers arrange themselves similarly, but each flower is attached by a stem; chokecherry and fireweed are examples. In plants with umbels, such as cow parsnip, the flower stems fan up from a single base like a sprung umbrella. A corymb is a flattish cluster in which the flower stems arise from different points along the stalk; spiraea is a lovely example. Flower heads are short, compact inflorescences such as occur in dandelions.

spots, from sage flats all the way up to sunny slopes at 7,000 feet.

The plant is composed of 1 or more flattened oval pads 2 to 5 inches long. Large, waxy, yellow or sometimes pink flowers bloom in early spring from the tops of the spiny pads, or cladodes. Blooms often last only 1 day and give way to roughly pear-shaped fruits.

As a way of saving water, prickly pears photosynthesize through their skin instead of growing large leaves for that function. Also unlike regular green plants, the stomata, or breathing pores, are open at night instead of during the day. This saves even more precious moisture.

Indigenous peoples split open the red fruit of the "hunger cactus," scraped away the seeds, and dried the pulp in the sun. Because of its gelatinous nature, prickly pear makes great jelly or candy. It was also used to thicken soups. Early peoples were also said to rub the peeled stem like aloe on wounds, and freshly peeled stems were rubbed over paint to fix color on hides.

The journals of Lewis and Clark reported that the prickly pear was "one of the beauties as well as the greatest pests of the plains." **Y, T, R**

ROCKY MOUNTAIN IRIS

There's no mistaking Rocky Mountain iris. The 1- to 2-foot-tall *Iris missouriensis* is the

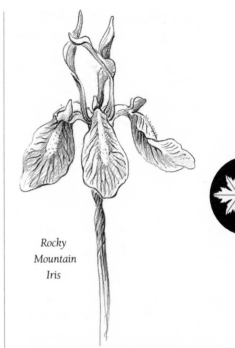

Rocky Mountain Iris

only member of the *Iris* genus in the region. Also called blue flag, fleur-de-lis, snake lily, and water flag, the plant has elegant, lavender blue flowers with dark blue veins. Three large, petal-like sepals droop down while 3 smaller center petals stand erect. Several swordlike leaves may grow out from the base or from the stem. This perennial has an irregularly shaped rootstock that contains the poison irisin, a substance that can cause violent purging in an unlucky consumer. Or worse. Some indigenous peoples apparently ground iris roots and used them in a mixture with animal bile to create a poison coating for arrows that caused death in humans within 3 to 7 days, even if the wound was slight.

Wherever there's blue flag, there's water. Look for this May-to-July bloomer in wet meadows or along streamsides all the way to 9,000 feet. The plant can also grow on hillsides and other drier places if there has been plenty of spring moisture. **G, Y, T, R**

SEGO LILY

One of the common names for this lovely lily, star tulip, conjures the right image. Picture a tall, slender stalk topped by a single showy blossom of 3 creamy white petals. Inside the flower of the sego lily (*Calochortus nuttallii*) is a dark purple mark at the base of each petal. Another evocative common name, mariposa lily, comes from the Spanish word for butterfly. (Although the name mariposa is sometimes used interchangeably with sego, the true mariposa lily is actually *C. gunnisonii*.)

Look for the sego lily in June and early July on dry plains and low-elevation hillsides, often in the company of sagebrush. In valley and mountain habitats, keep an eye out for one of the region's similar-looking species

Sego Lily

of *Calochortus,* including the true mariposa lily.

The sego lily could also be called Mormon lily. During the fall of 1848, when hordes of crickets damaged crops, many pioneering Mormons were saved from starvation by this plant's edible bulb. In remembrance of that harsh history, the state of Utah declared this its state flower.

Sego lilies were important to hungry people long before settlers came West. The crisp, sweet, nutritious bulb, about the size of a walnut, can be eaten raw or cooked. Native Americans commonly made bread from the starchy meal of the ground bulb. Bears and rodents also favor the tubers. **T, R**

SKY PILOT

Think of sky pilot as nature's way of reminding you to stay on the path in subalpine and alpine areas. If you shortcut the trail and step on this lovely flower, its skunky stink will trail you the rest of the day.

Polemonium viscosum is common in alpine meadows, boulder fields, and other open, rocky places in the Rocky Mountains, usually above timberline between 9,000 and 12,000 feet. *Viscosum* refers to the sticky, gland-covered sepals and bracts below the flowers that are responsible for the skunky smell. The flowers themselves produce a flowery aroma attractive to flying pollinators— but that won't be the fragrance to win out should you trample this plant.

In the phlox family, sky pilot begins blooming in June, with some late bloomers lingering into August. Showy, funnel-like, violet-blue to purple flowers form a compact cluster at the end of a 6- to 8-inch stem. Tiny oval leaves crowd along flowerless stalks surrounding the main stem.

This plant is also known as Jacob's ladder, but that name is

• THE IMPORTANCE OF PLANTS TO NATIVE CULTURES •

It's common to think of meat as being the primary food of early Native Americans, but plants were extremely significant to the survival and culture of indigenous Rocky Mountain peoples. Ethnobotanists such as Jeff Hart, author of *Montana Native Plants and Early Peoples,* have recorded a portion of that botanical heritage through extensive interviews with Native American elders and herbalists.

As Hart reminds us, Indians found food in berries, seeds, and nuts. They dug roots and bulbs, cut stems and shoots, and peeled bark from trees to get at the sweet inner layers. In addition to food, plants provided spices and healed injuries and illnesses.

Some plants, notes Hart, were considered to possess magical properties to ward off malefic spirits or summon beneficent ones, and so were used to scent sweat lodges and dwellings. Native peoples learned which plants could be smoked, which could be used as shampoo, and which functioned as insect repellent. They knew which plants to gather when horses were ailing, which ones to use for color dyes, and which shrubs to cut for the best arrow shafts.

The writings and historical accounts of ethnobotanists, explorers, Native Americans, mountain men, and settlers can serve to remind us of the rich natural stores under our very noses.

most correctly applied to *P. pulcherrimum,* one of the 10 species of polemoniums found in the Rocky Mountain region.

SPRING BEAUTY

Some of the most beloved plants and animals of the Rocky Mountains are cherished because they represent changing seasons; harbingers of spring are special favorites. Bluebirds are the flashy avian stars of that season; but while spring beauties are less conspicuous, they are no less gorgeous to winter-weary eyes.

Growing on a plant 4 to 8 inches tall, the dime-size, 5-petaled flowers are white or pink, with pink or purple veins.

The Handbook of Rocky Mountain Plants describes *Claytonia lanceolata*, a member of the purslane family, this way: "Leaves simple and entire, opposite or alternate; the flowers perfect." No matter that in botanical terms "perfect" means a bisexual flower with both pistil and stamen— "perfect" still describes how it feels to find the first one of the year. In early April flowers grow

• OBNOXIOUS NOXIOUS WEEDS •

Noxious weeds already infest nearly 20 million acres of federal public land and are continuing to spread through those lands at the startling rate of over 4,000 acres a day. (As defined by law, noxious weeds are plants of foreign origin that can directly or indirectly injure agriculture, navigation, fish or wildlife, or public health.)

Most noxious weeds were introduced, either intentionally as an ornamental plant or by accident, from Europe and Asia. Unfortunately, no natural insect enemies or diseases were imported along with them, so many of the invaders have thrived. Weed experts compare the spread to wildfire and warn that, if left uncontrolled, noxious weeds such as knapweed, Canada thistle, leafy spurge, yellow toadflax (butter-and-eggs), field bindweed, and yellow star thistle will dominate an area larger than the state of California by the year 2010.

This is a grim statistic for wildlife and native plants. When weeds take over an area, the number and variety of native insects, birds, and mammals is seriously diminished. Noxious weeds don't provide good forage for wildlife, and some are actually toxic. In western Montana, the invasion of spotted knapweed into areas of native bunchgrass has reduced winter forage available for elk as much as 50 percent to 90 percent. In habitats infested with leafy spurge, deer and bison use dropped 80 percent. This pushes more animals into noninfested sites, increasing grazing stress on weed-free range. Weeds don't just affect herbivores: seed-eating birds and rodents may not find weed seeds palatable, and the plants may not offer the kind of nesting or safety cover to which Rocky Mountain animals have become adapted. ➤

continues on page 170

• OBNOXIOUS NOXIOUS WEEDS *cont.* •

continued from page 169

Native plant communities in Glacier and Rocky Mountain National Parks, in the Bob Marshall Wilderness of Montana, and in other special places around the region are being seriously threatened by noxious weeds. In South Dakota, leafy spurge spread so far throughout the Altamont Prairie Preserve that the Nature Conservancy is no longer managing the land as a native prairie. Instead, a study is being conducted on ways to control spurge. Obviously, noxious weeds are an environmental concern, not simply an aesthetic issue—although it is certainly painful to watch a hillside of spring beauty, balsamroot, Indian paintbrush, and other native wildflowers and grasses being replaced by a monocultural expanse of weeds.

Weed seeds are disseminated by birds and wild animals as well as by humans. Some private landowners have considered closing their lands to fishing, hunting, and hiking because of the spread of noxious weeds. Learn to identify weeds so that you won't be an unwitting agent of their insidious expansion. Avoid driving or walking through weed patches, and don't pick a flower you can't identify. Many weeds are interesting-looking or pretty, and new infestations are caused when people take a souvenir tumbleweed or pick a knapweed bouquet in Montana and then throw it out in Colorado. Tumbleweeds carry seeds, and some wilted weed bouquets can develop roots directly from plant parts, even after weeks of use as a decoration.

Identification brochures and sometimes advice are available through county agricultural extension offices, the U.S. Forest Service, Bureau of Land Management, and state Departments of Agriculture.

---

in the moist soil of low elevation foothills and meadows; later, as snow retreats and the ground warms, higher up on mountain slopes and in alpine meadows. Early May marks the height of the flowering season at lower altitudes; mid-July is the peak for higher altitudes.

For early peoples, spring beauties meant more than a visual thrill. The highly edible and nutritious plants provided some of the first fresh foods after a long winter of meat and dried food stocks. The starchy, tuberlike corms (the thick, fleshy underground part of a stem) could be up to 1½ inches in diameter and were eaten raw or boiled. The raw corms have been described as having a "pleasant radishlike taste." Boiled tubers are reported to have the taste and texture of baked potatoes. Some Indian tribes came to call spring beauty "Indian potato," because the corm put them in mind of the introduced domestic potato.

Wildlife also appreciates spring beauty—particularly grizzly bears, which relish the tubers. Rodents also eat the corms, and the plant is grazed by deer, elk, and bighorn sheep. **G, Y, T, R**

WOOD NYMPH

The wood nymph has been called one of the most charming flowers of Rocky Mountain spruce forests. The ½- to 1-inch, white, waxy flower looks as if it belongs at the funeral of a fairy king, or perhaps the christening of an elfin babe. Its 5-petaled head nods slightly atop a bare, 2- to 4-inch-tall stem, with a fat, pineapple-shaped pistil resting in the center of the flower. A cluster of thin, roundish leaves encircles the base. Look for the widely distributed wood nymph in the moist soils of spruce, fir, and lodgepole forests in the montane and subalpine zones of the Rockies.

Most texts place this plant in the genus *Pyrola,* while a few others separate it into the *Moneses* genus, but everyone seems to agree on *uniflora* as a species name. A member of the wintergreen family, wood nymph often grows on rotting wood. The pyrolas are considered to be the "missing link" between green plants and such nongreen plants as pinedrops *(Pterospora andromedea)* and Indian pipe *(Monotropa uniflora).* Even though the leaves of wood nymph are

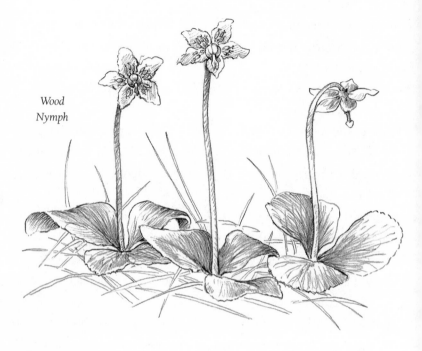

*Wood
Nymph*

green, you'll sense there's something different about this plant as soon as you see it.

Naturalists say that many individual pyrolas apparently hover at the edge of "nongreenness," wherein the plant doesn't photosynthesize, but instead gets its food by partnering with certain fungi to channel nutrients from other green plants. This ability allows pyrola to live deeper in the forest, where lack of light suppresses the growth of normal green plants.

G, R

· T H R E E ·

NATURAL FEATURES

NATURAL FEATURES

The Rocky Mountains are a weather machine. When moist air flowing from the west hits the mountains, all manner of interesting things are set in motion, among them rain, wind, snow, and stacks and stacks of clouds. The entries in the first part of this section explore the weather- and sky-related phenomena that give the Rocky Mountain region its split personality. Nothing typifies this more than a summer day that starts off calm and clear, only to build into a crashing thunderstorm by afternoon.

Features of the landscape, and the forces that created them, are the focus of the second part of this section. The Rockies wouldn't be here without the action of plate tectonics—a process that was still mere hypothesis in the 1960s. You may want to read "Plate Tectonics" before you dive into "Mountain Building."

If you think geology is without intrigue or excitement, be sure to read the entry on the Burgess Shale. Located in the Canadian Rockies not too far north of the border, this is arguably one of the most important fossil discoveries of all time, even though the animals there predated the more charismatic dinosaurs by millions of years.

Minerals and metals, glaciers, rocks, and rivers; the Rocky Mountain Trench and the Yellowstone Hot Spot: inanimate objects perhaps, but compelling features that give the Rockies a face and foundation. And, after all, the landscape shapes the life.

AVALANCHE

Hopefully you won't see any avalanches, but even in summer you can keep an eye out for their tracks. When driving or hiking through the Rockies, look for avalanche chutes—

Avalanche

conspicuous open slots running down through forested slopes. Avalanche tracks tend to run along gullies rather than on ridges. Don't confuse the slots with logging clear-cuts, which are more rectangular or horizontal.

Frequency of slides determines the type of vegetation growing in avalanche chutes. If slides are infrequent, fast-growing aspen trees may have time to colonize the open area. Limber pines are another tree you might find in an avalanche zone. In active chutes, you'll find only low shrubs, wildflowers, and grasses.

About 140 people a year in the United States are caught in avalanches; odds are 17 of those people will be killed. Colorado has the highest avalanche death rate, followed closely by Washington and Utah. The good news is that we know enough about avalanches that no one needs to be caught with their beacon down (backcountry recreationists wear radio transmitters that can help rescuers locate them under the snow).

Some of the key factors that determine avalanche danger are steepness of slope, amount and type of new snow, temperature, wind, and condition of existing snowpack. Throughout the winter, each snowfall contributes a new layer to the snowpack. Some storms produce light, powdery snow; others lay down wetter, heavier layers. In between snowfalls, wind and sun put a crust on each new layer.

Temperatures in the snowpack are typically coldest near the top surface and warmest near the ground surface. When there is a large difference between the two surface temperatures, ice crystals near the bottom become weak and are susceptible to collapsing. When weak crystals collapse, they leave the overlying slab of snow in danger of slipping.

Fully 80 percent of all avalanches occur during or just after a snowfall. Danger is generally greatest when it snows an inch or more per hour. Avalanches are most common on slopes of 30 to 60 degrees, although a slide of very wet snow on a gently sloping beginner's ski hill in Japan killed 7 people.

Throughout the winter, avalanche experts take snowpack core samples to observe the condition of the layers and evaluate risk. Don't go into steep backcountry unless you are fully educated and prepared. As they say in *The Avalanche Book,* "Avoiding avalanches is easier than surviving them." (See Snow)

CLOUDS

The Rocky Mountains are a veritable cloud laboratory. On any clear blue summer morning, keep an eye on the sky to see what develops. Cloud watchers won't be disappointed; over 80 percent of summer days in the Rockies are at least partly cloudy. In winter, clouds can cover the high country for days on end.

Basically, clouds form when moist air is cooled. In the mountains, air is often cooled through a process known as orographic (mountain-related)

lifting. Air cools as it rises up a slope. When it cools to the point that it can no longer hold moisture as a vapor, the moisture condenses as a cloud or fog, depending on how high the air rose.

Clouds are lumped into 2 basic groups: cumulus, also known as heaped, or vertical, clouds; and stratus, or horizontal, layered clouds. Cumulus clouds result

Cumulus Clouds

While you're up at cloud level on some Rocky Mountain peak, be aware of dangers beyond the obvious avalanches and hailstorms. Acute mountain sickness (AMS) is an altitude-related illness.

On a gradual climb or drive, most people barely notice the effects of altitude gain—colder air, more intense sun, less oxygen, and decreased barometric pressure. But above 7,000 feet, our bodies have a significantly harder time absorbing oxygen into the bloodstream. Decreased oxygen in the blood combined with decreased air pressure is potentially damaging to blood vessels and blood cells in the lungs and brain. Warning signs include headache, dizziness, racing pulse, irregular breathing, puffiness in the hands and face, nausea, and a feeling of weakness. The symptoms—which some people report as low as 5,000 feet—usually disappear as soon as the affected person moves to a lower elevation or, if symptoms aren't severe, has had a chance to acclimate. While symptoms persist, the person should take in lots of uncaffeinated fluids, get plenty of rest, practice relaxed breathing, and take aspirin for headache. Stay alert for signs of serious trouble. In the event of a watery cough or severe headache, a pulse rate exceeding 120 beats per minute, gurgling sounds emanating from the lungs, loss of coordination and balance, or nausea lasting more than a few hours, seek a lower elevation immediately.

Gaining elevation too quickly is the main cause, although dehydration, cold, and fatigue can all exacerbate AMS. The condition is more of a serious concern to mountaineers than to tourists, but even casual travelers can feel the effects, especially if flying into high-altitude cities from sea level.

A random sampling of Rocky Mountain elevations (in feet): Estes Park, Colorado, 7,522; Loveland Pass, Colorado, 11,992; Pikes Peak, Colorado, 14,110; Big Sky, Montana, 6,970; Logan Pass, Glacier National Park, Montana, 6,664; Jackson Hole, Wyoming, 6,200; the Grand Teton, Wyoming, 13,770; Yellowstone Lake, Yellowstone National Park, Wyoming, 7,733; Stanley, Idaho, 6,661; Sun Valley, Idaho, 5,736.

---

from rising, unstable air. They are dense, independent clouds that mushroom up from flattish bottoms, looking like giant pieces of popcorn. Stratus clouds, on the other hand, are products of stable air and spread across the sky like a wet, wool blanket.

When precipitation is associated with a cloud, some form of the word "nimbus" is tacked on, such as nimbostratus or cumulonimbus. Similarly, when a cloud is at 18,000 feet or higher, some form of the word "cirrus" is applied, as in cirrocumulus or cirrostratus. Cirrus, from the Latin for "tendril," also stands alone. Cirrus clouds are often called mare's tails and appear as delicate tufts, streaks, or plumes high in the sky.

So, clouds are basically a mix of cumulus, stratus, nimbus, cirrus, and alto—another altitude descriptor. For hard-core cloud aficionados, clouds can be further broken down into species and varieties. Some of the most interesting to watch for in the Rockies are the lenticular species and mammata and virga varieties.

Lenticular clouds are especially orographic. Shaped like lenses, almonds, or flying saucers, these streamlined clouds are formed by air currents moving over the mountains in waves.

Mammatiform clouds look like fat teats and are most often seen hanging from the dark undersurface of a thundercloud.

Virga appears as streaks of rain or ice crystals wisping down from a cloud but evaporating before reaching the ground. (See Hail; Thunderstorm)

HAIL

Hail is a specialty of thunderstorms, and thunderstorms are a spectacular specialty of the Rocky Mountains. Some higher-elevation locations may experience 20 or more hailstorms during the summer season. The high plains adjacent to the eastern front of the Rockies are called Hail Alley and experience more frequent hailstorms than any other location in North America.

Oftentimes, you can hear a hailstorm rattling and hissing toward you as hailstones hit roofs, rocks, or roads. If you're in a vehicle when the bombardment arrives, the noise can be deafening.

Hailstones range from the size of a pea to the size of a softball; larger ones can cause extensive damage to crops, gardens, buildings, and vehicles. After a sudden summer hailstorm, watch for pickup trucks slowly patrolling roads adjacent to cultivated fields as farmers and ranchers check for damage. Damage can be exacerbated by a strong wind that often accompanies the falling column of hail.

Violent updrafts and downdrafts within storm clouds are behind this climatological hooliganism. A hailstone begins to form when a tiny pellet of ice or small particulate gets caught in a powerful updraft. As it's pulled through the super-cold water droplets in the cloud, it adds layers of ice. As the stone hits a downdraft, it's pulled back through the frigid droplets, adding yet more layers. The growing stone rides these cycles of updrafts and downdrafts until it gets tossed out the top of an updraft, or becomes too heavy to remain aloft, or the updraft weakens. New evidence indicates that hailstones may also grow by holding steady in the updraft, gathering the super-cooled drops that strike them.

In its early stages, hail may fall as graupel, or soft hail. These opaque white pellets, up to $1/5$ inch in diameter, have a snowlike structure, but can bounce on hard surfaces. "Small hail" may be the same size as graupel, but is denser and has at least a partially glazed surface. When pellets are at least $1/5$ inch in diameter and consist of translucent, layered ice, they can officially be called hail.

The column of hail falling from a single thunderstorm cell is called a hailshaft. Hailshafts may sweep along at 30 to 35 mph, occasionally reaching speeds of 60 mph. The path of ground battered by a hailshaft is called the hailstreak. Normally, hailstreaks are about 5 miles long and about 100 feet to 2 miles wide. All the hailstreaks of a storm are known collectively as the hailswath.

The basic requirements for producing hail are strong vertical air currents and a low freezing level aloft. Rare in the tropics, in polar regions, and near coastal areas, hail occurs most frequently between 30 and 60 degrees latitude (roughly Big Bend National Park in Texas to the southern border of the Yukon and Northwest Territories of Canada). In the tropics, freezing levels are at such high altitudes that hail melts before it reaches the ground. In the far north, updrafts never build enough strength to produce hail because the air is too cold.

Although word-of-mouth accounts from the 18th and 19th centuries report death by hail, only 2 deaths have been authenticated by the National Weather Service. The most recent was July 30, 1979, when an infant was killed by hail at Fort Collins, Colorado. Denver has also experienced severe hailstorms; on July 13, 1984, hail broke car windshields and caused nearly $200 million in property damage. Another storm on July 11, 1990, caused about $600 million in damage to the Denver area. (See Clouds; Thunderstorm)

RAINBOW

A marriage of opposites begets the rainbow: sun plus rain. In the Rockies, localized rain showers sweeping across big views make the region a perfect place for the wedding.

To set the stage, you need a curtain of rain on one side and a shining sun on the other. When sunlight strikes individual rain droplets, the light is bent, or refracted, and each color of the spectrum takes a slightly different angle through the water. As the light waves hit the back of each drop, they bounce back toward the sun, still separated into individual colors.

Even if you watch a rainbow while holding hands with your sweetie, each of you will see a

• CREPUSCULAR RAYS AND SILVER LININGS •

The partly cloudy Rocky Mountain days that produce thunderstorms and rainbows also produce crepuscular rays. These are dramatic rays of light that appear to radiate from the sun like spread fingers. They are created when scattered or broken clouds or a mountain range partially obstruct the path of sunlight. Light rays are made more visible by the presence of atmospheric dust or water vapor.

A silver lining is often seen along the edges of cumulus clouds associated with crepuscular rays. This narrow band of iridescence is created when light scatters from cloud droplets at the less dense, outer part of the cloud.

different manifestation. Light travels in a straight line, so what you see is your own, private rainbow show.

Glories are a related phenomenon. In the mountains, usually when the sun is low, a glory can appear as a faintly colored rainbow around the shadow of your own head. Watch for this magical sight when your back is to the sun and your shadow falls on mist or fog. If several people are standing together, each will see only the halo around his or her own head—a function of the above-mentioned light dispersal, not karma.

SNOW

In the Rocky Mountains, it can—and will—snow at any time of year. The greatest 24-hour snowfall recorded in North America happened April 14–15, 1921, when 76 inches fell on Silver Lake, just west of the continental divide in San Juan County, Colorado.

No inventor could have developed a better snow-making machine than the Rockies. The mountains form a gigantic barrier to air masses moving east from the Pacific Ocean, forcing air to rise and cool. Cool air can't hold on to its moisture, which it drops in the form of snow or rain. Snowfall is the greatest on the high peaks, some of which receive 200 to 400 inches of snow annually, roughly the equivalent of 20 to 40 inches of rain. (As a rule of thumb, 10 to 12 inches of new-fallen snow equals about 1 inch of water.)

Snowflakes are aggregates of ice crystals, whose size and form are determined by temperature, humidity, wind conditions, and even barometric pressure. Large, elaborate crystals form when temperatures and humidity are on the high side, while the small, simple crystals of polar regions form when temperatures and humidity are extremely low. For two snow crystals to be exactly alike, let alone flakes, they would have to form in precisely identical conditions and collect the very same number of water vapor molecules. So it's quite safe to say that, yes, no two snowflakes are alike.

Rocky Mountain skiers have adopted a lingo to describe different snow conditions, including glop, fluff, crud, sugar, corn, and cement—and, of course, that most irresistible condition of all, powder.

Besides providing recreation for humans, snow provides insulating cover for plants and animals, protecting them from wind and freezing temperatures. A good snowpack is also essential to the well-being of mountain and valley ecosystems, providing water through the dry months as snow slowly melts and feeds soil, creeks, and rivers. Snowpack accounts for up to about 75 percent of annual runoff. Healthy forests and meadows, with their extensive root systems, help regulate the spring and summer runoff, allowing a slow, sustained release of water instead of torrential floods.

While on winter outings in the high country, you might see a number of snow-related phenomena. Snow banners are plumes of snow blowing off

Snow Banner

mountaintops. Rare snow garlands look like ropes of snow draping off fences or between trees. Both green and red (or watermelon) snow are caused by microscopic algae. While you're watching for garlands, banners, and watermelon, don't forget to also watch out for avalanches. (See Avalanche)

SUN DOG

Next time you see a halo around the sun, look to see if the Rocky Mountain celestial watchdogs are out as well. Sun dogs are luminous spots of subtly colored light sitting on the halo on the right- and left-hand sides of Sol. (You can see the halo and sun dogs with your peripheral vision; of course, you should never look at the sun directly.) If conditions are right, you may see a tail—a short, horizontal line of white light—on each dog too. Sun dogs are also called mock suns because they look somewhat like duplicate suns flanking the real one.

Sun dogs and the haloes on which they sit are caused by the refraction (bending) and sometimes reflection of sunlight by ice crystals in the atmosphere. A halo isn't as colorful as a rainbow, but the pale ring does shine reddish toward the inside and blue on the outside.

Sun haloes are always about the same size, because light consistently bends at a 22-degree angle off 6-sided ice crystals. If you make a fist and, with your arm outstretched, put your thumb on the sun (without looking at it!) as if you were pressing in a thumbtack, the outer edge of the halo should be just outside the edge of your fist.

THUNDERSTORM

Forget bears and marauding moose—thunderstorms are one of the most serious dangers to summer hikers and climbers in the Rocky Mountains. The best protection against lightning strikes and the life-threatening chill of hypothermia is simple good judgment.

Thunderstorm season begins in late spring, triggered by warming ground temperatures, and lasts through the summer. When the ground warms, it heats the air, causing the air to rise and cool. Because cool air holds less moisture than warm air, water begins to condense, forming clouds.

Anyone spending time in the Rockies learns that clouds tend to begin forming over the mountains in late morning and intensify into the early afternoon as the ground

Thunderstorm

• LIGHTNING, THUNDER, AND SAFETY •

Lightning is basically a big electric spark between 2 oppositely charged points. It develops within a growing cumulonimbus cloud as a predominantly positive charge at the top and negative charge at the lower end of the cloud.

When the charges build to their full potential, a discharge occurs between the 2 opposite forces. Most lightning stays within a cloud or between clouds, with only about 20 percent of discharges happening between a cloud and the ground.

Cloud-to-ground lightning begins with a negative discharge from the cloud known as a leader. When the leader strikes downward, a return stroke flows up from the ground to meet it at about 422 million feet per second, discharging energy that is seen as a flash of light.

Thunder is generated as the lightning discharge heats gases in the atmosphere to about 18,000°F, causing the air to expand violently. Resultant waves of pressure and compression cause the noise. Lightning and thunder happen simultaneously, but since light travels so much faster than sound, we see the lightning first. It takes about 5 seconds for thunder to travel 1 mile, so to estimate how far away lightning is, count the number of seconds between the lightning flash and the thunder and divide by 5.

Ground discharges that occur after lightning strikes can be even more dangerous than the strike itself. As lightning develops, the ground becomes positively charged. As the ground tries to return to the equilibrium of its normal negative charge, it disperses electrical currents that can flash between objects such as people and trees within a 100-foot radius of the strike.

About 300 people in the United States die of lightning strikes each year. If you see a storm approaching, take cover in plenty of time, as lightning can travel well ahead of the storm. Get off ridges and seek shelter in a cluster of small trees instead of under one large tree. Avoid gullies with water. Out in the open, find the driest low spot and crouch on both feet (one, if possible), arms around your knees, on a pad or some extra clothing to insulate yourself from the ground. Members of a party should stay at least 30 feet from one another, and be prepared to administer CPR and first aid should one of the group be hit. Avoid shallow caves or overhangs. If you're riding, dismount and crouch away from the horse.

continues to heat up. (Solar radiation is intense at high elevations, heating the surface relatively quickly.) Thunderstorm prime time is usually between 4 P.M. and 6 P.M.

While you're out and about, watching wildlife or reading rivers, don't forget to check out the clouds. What looks like a little puffy cotton ball at 10 A.M. can be a towering mass by 2 P.M. A developing thundercloud is white with a flat bottom. When fully developed, the top of the cloud may reach the stratosphere, 7 miles up. The cloud turns gray with condensing moisture and may take on an anvil shape. Hikers need to pay particular attention at this point and look for virga—wispy precipitation draping from the cloud but not quite reaching the ground. Virga, which means "veil" in Spanish, foretells the likely onset of lightning. Ideally, hikers should be off exposed peaks, ridges, and tundra slopes before virga appears.

The fully developed cumulonimbus thundercloud is an entire weather system unto itself, capable of producing rain, hail, snow, thunder, lightning, and high winds. In late July of 1976, an extremely violent thunderstorm stalled just east of Estes Park, Colorado, dumping 10 inches of rain and hail over a few hours. The resulting flood killed at least 139 people as it ripped through Big Thompson Canyon. (See Clouds; Hail)

WILDFIRE

The Yellowstone fires of 1988 brought wildfire and fire management policies of the Rocky Mountain West into the public consciousness. Over 700,000 acres burned—more acres than had burned in the previous 116 years. During those years, natural fire cycles had been suppressed in the West, leading to a tremendous fuel load in the form of dead trees, leaf litter, and dry shrubs and grasses.

You can still see the standing, dead, charred trees left from the Yellowstone fires, but new growth is occurring. In the Rockies, fire is the most important natural recycler of the nutrients that keep ecosystems productive.

In the last couple of decades, forest managers have begun to accept the need for fire, and there is an attempt to manage fires now, rather than completely suppress them.

There are 2 basic types of wildfire: crown fires and ground, or surface, fires. Even though crown fires are fueled by ground litter, the fire moves across the tops of trees. These are the most devastating fires, creating their own hellish winds and killing virtually all trees, shrubs, and herbaceous plants.

Surface fires occur when there isn't a huge fuel load covering the forest floor, or when the ground is relatively moist. These fires burn only litter, seedlings, saplings, shrubs, grasses, and wildflowers. Usually, mature trees are merely singed. Ground fires move slowly and are relatively easy to control.

The only way to avoid catastrophic crown fires is to allow periodic surface fires to clear up fuels. Prescribed surface fires are now part of forest management.

Prescribed fires are really nothing new. As far as we know, all Native American cultures used fire to improve grazing for wildlife and foraging for people. Lewis and Clark also described how some Indian tribes used fire for driving bison.

An extremely hot fire can eat through ground litter and actually burn the soil, causing regrowth to be delayed, but most fires leave the soil renewed with recycled minerals and exposed to sunlight— perfect conditions for regeneration. In a spruce forest, the first plants to reappear are aggressive and tolerant of dry soil and full sun. Fireweed and wild geraniums are among the first forbs (nonwoody, seed-producing plants other than grasses) to show up. Grasses and other forbs follow. After those come woody shrubs and trees such as chokecherry and aspen. Next in line are the pioneering conifers, including lodgepole pine, subalpine fir, and Douglas-fir. The shade-tolerant spruce grows next, eventually taking over to create the climax forest. Some researchers say climax spruce forests go to bogs if fire doesn't interrupt the cycle once again.

Certain bird species, including great gray owls, mountain bluebirds, and woodpeckers, often do quite well after a fire, even experiencing population increases. Populations of carnivorous mammals requiring large territories, such as lynx and wolverine, may require decades to recover. Generally, however, fire is good for wildlife in the long term because it results in plant diversity and creates a patchwork of different habitats to support a wider variety of animals and birds

WINDS

Wind is the "Invisible Man" of the Rocky Mountains. He will rearrange your deck furniture, blow dust in your eyes, push a tree down across your road, and raise whitecaps around your canoe. But he's lived here as long as the mountains, so there's not much use complaining.

Most commonly, winds are from the west, generated over the Pacific Ocean. It's nearly always windy above timberline, especially on ridges and peaks. During the winter of 1981 an anemometer (wind gauge) on top of Longs Peak in Rocky Mountain National Park recorded a gust of 201 mph, nearly 3 times hurricane force. Other records from the park show an average summer wind speed at the Alpine Tundra Museum of 20 mph with gusts up to 80 mph. Many alpine plants have adapted to their windy environment by becoming short and developing hair or fuzz to trap warmth and moisture.

Although the prevailing winds are westerly (blowing eastward), mountainous topography can alter wind direction, channeling air down canyons or up steep

On October 24, 1997, in the Routt National Forest north of Steamboat Springs, Colorado, 120-mph winds blasted through a forest of Engelmann spruce and subalpine fir, knocking down 6 million trees in a swath 25 miles long and several miles wide. The 20,000-acre blowdown was the largest of its kind in the Rockies, and possibly the most extensive blowdown of spruce anywhere in the United States. Most of the trees were 200 to 350 years old and up to 100 feet tall.

The storm was generated by freak winds from the east that spun off a massive low-pressure system over the Great Plains, crested the continental divide, and literally plowed down the trees. Some snapped off at the trunk, while others keeled over, exposing their root balls.

In places, the blow left impenetrable walls of timber 20 feet high. A few people witnessed the drama, including a group of hunters who found shelter in a sturdy log cabin; remarkably, no one was killed or seriously hurt. It took the hunters a day to cut their way out of the area with chain saws.

Making a stab at explaining the extensive damage to healthy trees, some experts surmised that, since prevailing winds are from the west, the trees' root systems hadn't grown in a way that would anchor them against such force from the east.

river valleys. A phenomenon known as valley wind may also change prevailing air currents. On sunny days, warm air moves up toward the head or top of the valley as a gentle breeze. At night, the air cools and becomes heavier, flowing back down the valley like an outgoing ocean tide.

The Invisible Man's brother, Chinook wind, lives on the lee, or east, side of the Rockies. When low pressure lies on one side of a mountain range and high pressure on the other, the low will suck air over the range. As it slips down the lee side, warming and drying as it goes, it may gather speed like an avalanche. The warm, dry Chinook wind can raise temperatures radically and nearly instantaneously. It has a greedy appetite for moisture and, in winter, can gobble up snow like cotton candy. Some Native Americans called this wind the "snow eater."

• G E O L O G Y & G E O G R A P H Y •

BASEMENT ROCK

The Rockies we know today first began uplifting only about 100 million years ago, making them quite young in the geological scheme of things. But thanks to the process of uplift and the force of erosion, you can lay your eyes on rock that was formed when bacteria were the only life forms on earth.

Granite, gneiss, and schist rocks are often referred to as "continental basement rock" because no other rocks lie underneath them in the earth's crust layer. Although no one has drilled all the way through, it is thought that basement rock goes all the way down to the mantle. Granite, gneiss, and schist essentially make up the core of the Rocky Mountains.

Where overlying layers of sedimentary or volcanic rock have eroded away (layers sometimes originally thousands of feet thick), this beautiful basement rock is exposed to view. In the northern Rockies, exposed basement rocks are thought to be about 2.7 *billion* years old.

Granites are massive, unbanded rocks of light gray or pink. Gneiss and schist are banded and sometimes folded, and are usually gray, pink, and dark brown. In these basement rocks, you can usually see black spikes of the mineral hornblende and shiny flakes of black mica. The pink and white minerals are most commonly feldspar and quartz.

When you find a swirl of banded gneiss, touch it and think

about the fact that this gorgeous metamorphic rock is formed of ancient sediments and volcanic deposits from the earth's earliest days.

You'll notice exposed basement rock throughout the Rockies. Some of the more obvious places to find Precambrian banded gneiss are in outcrops high on the Beartooth Plateau of Montana and at Rocky Mountain National Park along Trail Ridge Road. The Sharkstooth and Hayden Spire are both made of gneiss and its close, metamorphic cousin, schist. (See Rocky Mountain Rock)

BURGESS SHALE

During the 1909 field season, Charles Doolittle Walcott, paleontologist and secretary of the Smithsonian Institution, noticed shiny black film on some broken rock slabs high in the Canadian Rockies near Golden, in southern British Columbia. Upon inspection, he saw that the film was the flattened fossils of soft-bodied animals—creatures without shells or skeletons.

Walcott had discovered the first deposit of fossilized animals from the Cambrian period, the time beginning about 600 million years ago when life began to evolve from single-celled bacteria into multicelled organisms recognizable as animals. Scientists refer to the diversification of life during that 100-million-year-long period as the Cambrian Explosion. (The entire 4 billion years of earth history preceding the Cambrian is called simply the Precambrian era.)

Naturalist and author Stephen Jay Gould has called the Burgess Shale the most important fossil deposit ever found. For all its importance, the site itself is modest, though perched in a breathtaking setting. The Burgess Shale is an outcrop of shale rock about 200 feet long and about 8 feet tall lying exposed high on the flank of Mount Stephen on the east side of Burgess Pass.

• CREATURES FROM THE CAMBRIAN •

Most of the fossil animals of the Burgess Shale were arthropods. The phylum Arthropoda is a huge group of invertebrates that includes insects, arachnids, crustaceans, and other animals with segmented bodies and jointed limbs, at least 1 pair of which is specialized as jaws. But the Burgess fossil fauna also includes a great array of other kinds of animals. Many of the fossil species are thought to be ancestors of current living animals, though at least 20 of the 120 species identified were difficult to place into any modern group.

Wiwaxia is one example. This 1- to 2-inch-long marine creature looked like half a walnut shell completely covered with plated armor and bearing 2 rows of spearlike spikes along its back. As with most species of this time, *Wiwaxia* had no eyes.

Hallucigenia is one of the more notorious Burgess Shale animals. This creature, named for its "bizarre and dreamlike quality," looked like a long-legged caterpillar with sets of long, pointed spines running the length of its back. *Hallucigenia* was originally portrayed upside down and backward, until more complete specimens were found to help paleontologists better visualize it.

Perhaps the most compelling fossil is that of *Pikaia*. First described as a worm, *Pikaia* is now thought to be the earliest known representative of the Chordata phylum, to which human beings also belong. This sea creature looked like a flattened snake with the head of a snail and a tail expanded into a fin. Although *Pikaia* is not a full-fledged vertebrate, it is thought that all modern vertebrates branched off from animals such as this.

Trilobites, the most famous fossil arthropods, make up only a fraction of the Burgess fossils—although a world-famous trilobite quarry is located on a mountain near the Burgess Shale.

Hallucigenia

Pikaia

Mountain goats watch from the sidelines as researchers continue to investigate the site.

About 120 Cambrian species were eventually described; all had lived in or on the mud of a shallow sea. The Burgess fauna provided a kind of Rosetta stone in deciphering Cambrian evolution. Based on the findings, it's thought that all the animal phyla in existence today, except possibly Bryozoa, arose during that time. (Phyla are the main divisions of the animal kingdom, based on body design; vertebrates, arthropods, and mollusks are examples of different animal phyla.)

It's quite unusual for soft-bodied animals to be preserved as fossils. In the fortunate case of the Burgess Shale, a mud slide apparently swept the animals down to the foot of an underwater reef, where a lack of oxygen kept them from decaying. The reef provided a sort of pressure shadow, which kept the fossils from deforming beyond recognition.

Similar deposits have now been discovered in China and Greenland, but the Burgess Shale remains the *Lagerstätten* of Cambrian fossils. *Lagerstätten* is a German term referring to a fossil lode that yields exceptional fossils. There are about 100 such key locations in the world, preserving extraordinary snapshots of different evolutionary periods.

CONTINENTAL DIVIDE

A nearly continuous 10,000-mile-long chain of mountains snakes all the way from Alaska through South America. The section of that cordillera that runs from Canada into the southwest United States, we call the Rocky Mountains. Along the highest peaks and ridges of the Rockies runs a zigzagging imaginary line, the Continental Divide.

Unlike so many of our named boundaries—state and county lines, voting and school districts, national parks, speed zones—this division takes its definition straight from geography. Streams on the east side of the Continental Divide eventually flow into the Gulf of Mexico. On the west side, streams flow into the Pacific Ocean or Gulf of California. There is no equivalent Continental Divide in the eastern United States.

The Continental Divide runs through Glacier, Yellowstone, and Rocky Mountain National Parks; in fact, for most of its 3,000 miles, the Continental Divide is on public, federal land.

Generally speaking, the divide trends from northwest to southeast. It does, however, run east-west in places to follow a dogleg in some mountain range or another, so a Rockies road trip may have you crossing and recrossing the divide several times. Yellowstone's Mammoth Hot Springs is on the east side of the divide, while directly south, Jackson Hole is on the west side.

The divide does more than simply separate east from west; it defines the nature of east-side and west-side ecosystems. That jutting cordillera catches clouds blowing in from the Pacific Ocean and squeezes out most of their moisture. Once past the peaks, air moving eastward is much drier.

Continental Divide

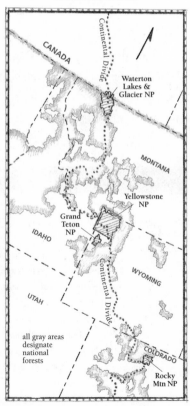

197

Notice how different vegetation is in the rain shadow on the east side of the divide compared with the wetter west side.

One of the most interesting places to cross the divide is Logan Pass in Glacier National Park. At 6,664 feet, the pass is relatively low, but there's a trail (rated as difficult) that follows the divide a number of miles to a glacial arête called the Garden Wall. Thanks to a ridge jutting out on the east slope of the divide at the Garden Wall, precipitation falling on the north side of that ridge, called the Hudson Bay Divide, feeds creeks that run into the Saskatchewan River system, which flows northeast to drain into Hudson Bay.

EARTHQUAKES

It's one thing to hear the somewhat abstract observation that the Rockies are still rising. But to put it another way—the northern Rockies are the second most seismically active region in all of North America, behind only California's San Andreas Fault zone.

Almost all of the mountain ranges that trend north-south in the region have faults running along their flanks. Some, including faults

• RICHTER AND MERCALLI •

The Richter scale, named after U.S. seismologist Charles Francis Richter (1900–1985), is an objective ranking of an earthquake's magnitude based on seismic waves. Magnitude is the measurable amount of energy an earthquake releases at its epicenter. Each number represents 31 times more energy than the number before. An earthquake measuring 2 on the Richter scale is barely noticeable, whereas a quake measuring 8 could flatten a city.

The Mercalli scale, named after Italian seismologist Giuseppe Mercalli (1850–1914), is a subjective ranking of an earthquake's intensity. On the modified Mercalli scale, an earthquake measuring 1 means "felt by few," whereas a quake of 12 means "damage total."

along the base of the Tetons, are still active. Others, quiet for some time, are thought to be inactive.

One of the strongest earthquakes in U.S. history occurred in Montana along the Red Canyon Fault in the Madison River Canyon. Shortly before midnight on August 17, 1959, the fault slipped, releasing an earthquake that registered 7.1 on the Richter scale and shook an 8-state region. Every town within a 100-mile radius suffered damage. In the canyon, 28 people died, buried under massive slides of debris. Another 250 recreationists were trapped overnight as sections of U.S. Highway 287 crumbled and fell into the Hebgen Lake reservoir. Several miles downstream from Hebgen Dam, earthquake debris formed another dam, creating Quake Lake, which still exists as a geologic memorial. There is also a human-made memorial in the canyon that is well worth the visit.

We think of mountain building as a slow process, but in that one night, the distance between the mountains and the canyon floor grew by 15 feet. The resultant, clifflike fault scarp is clearly visible; look for it at the base of the mountains on the north side of the road between Hebgen and Quake Lakes.

The earthquake also tilted Hebgen Lake. The south side was raised, leaving former lakeside cabins far from shore, while the north side dropped, causing cabins on that side to be flooded. Tremors created giant seiche waves in the lake, sending them sloshing over Hebgen Dam, which cracked, but didn't fail.

A more recent quake, near Challis, Idaho, also shook the entire northern Rockies region. On October 28, 1983, an earthquake registering 7.3 on the Richter scale caused the Big Lost River Range to rise over a foot, while the valley floor dropped over 4 feet. The 6-foot-high rocky scar, or fault scarp, created by that quake is also plainly visible, running for several miles along the base of the Big Lost River Range. Eyewitnesses saw the nearly instantaneous slippage. Several buildings in Challis collapsed, killing 2 children.

Water gushed in fountains from the valley floor for several days after the quake, and a silver mine in the area was flooded with water. Elsewhere, springs dried up for a few days and then ran with greater flows than they had previously. Even Old Faithful Geyser in Yellowstone was affected, erupting less frequently for a while.

GLACIERS

Geologic forces uplifted the northern Rockies; then ice-age glaciers sculpted, carved, gouged, rounded, shaped, rearranged, and polished the landscape into what we see today.

No one is really sure how many ice ages have come and gone, but the number is probably between 8 and 20. In the northern Rockies, one of the oldest we can trace is known as the Bull Lake glaciation, which probably occurred a little over 100,000 years ago. The most recent ice age, referred to as the Pinedale glaciation, ended about 12,000 years ago.

Ice sheets descended from British Columbia as far south as Coeur d'Alene in the panhandle of Idaho and covered about the northern third of Montana. Some mountain ranges were almost completely inundated, with only the very tallest peaks holding out above the frigid white fields. The northern end of the Flathead Valley in northwestern Montana was covered in ice more than a mile thick, even though the glacier ended just south of Flathead Lake. Icy fingers descended into major valleys, scouring out long, straight, north-south channels that became the Flathead, Mission, and Bitterroot Valleys of northwest Montana.

Taller or more southerly ranges in Idaho and Montana escaped

• ANATOMY OF A GLACIER •

Alpine glaciers, also known as valley glaciers and mountain glaciers, are fields of snow that accumulate in mountains when more snow falls than melts. You won't see many large glaciers in the Rocky Mountains, but you will see sculpted evidence of long-gone alpine glaciers nearly everywhere you look.

To oversimplify, glaciers collect rocky debris at their sides and bottom as freeze-thaw cycles loosen fragments from surrounding stone. As the glacier travels downward with gravity, the rocks act as a sort of rasp (look for scratch marks in exposed bedrock). As the glacier moves down, it carves and deposits a predictable series of topographical features. Think of the following as the trace fossils of extinct glaciers.

Arêtes mark where the head of the glacier was. This word comes from the French for "fish bone" and refers to a thin, knifelike ridge, usually found where cirques have formed back to back. *Cirques* look like bowls that have been gouged from near the mountain-top with an ice-cream scoop. They often cradle lakes, called tarns. *Horns* are pyramid-shaped peaks, formed when cirques have scooped ground away on 3 or more sides. *Hanging valleys*, formed by tributary, or side, glaciers, are high, small valleys that end abruptly, far above the main valley floor. You may see spectacular waterfalls cascading down from them. *Moraines* are the glacier's gravel dumps. Lateral moraines form like ridges along the sides of the glacier as rocks accumulate at the edges. When the glacier finally melts, its undercoat of rocks is exposed as a ground moraine, and the wall of rocks it had piled up at its foot is called the end, or terminal, moraine. *Erratics* are rocks and boulders—some the size of a house— that were deposited at their present position by a glacier. In the northern Rockies, any large, isolated boulder that's not attached to bedrock is most likely an erratic. You can easily see them out in the open, but it's especially amazing to come upon a large erratic in the forest, surrounded by trees.

total coverage by the ice sheet. An interesting comparison can be made from U.S. Highway 2, which follows the Kootenai River between Libby, Montana, and the Idaho line. The river separates the Purcell Mountains on the north from the Cabinet Mountains on the south. Ice nearly buried the Purcells, which now have a smoothly rounded look. The Cabinets weren't buried, but they did have large numbers of mountain glaciers, also

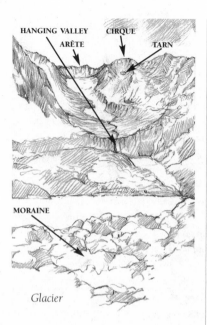

Glacier

confusingly known as valley glaciers. Those glaciers carved the Cabinets a rugged profile, in sharp contrast to the glacially rasped Purcells. Nearly the entire route of Highway 2 passes through valleys bearing evidence of extinct glaciers. Look for the telltale tailings of glaciers, called moraines, littered with glacially transported boulders. North of Highway 2, in Glacier National Park, some forest-covered lateral moraines are 2,000 feet high.

Although Rocky Mountain National Park was well south of the main ice sheet, ice-age conditions created glaciers in that region. During the Pinedale glaciation, up to 2,000 feet of ice filled the park's major valleys and marked the landscape with sharp ridges, U-shaped valleys, and bowl-like cirques. Today, the park holds only 5 small glaciers.

Don't expect to see world-class glaciers at Glacier National Park either—Glacier's original 90 glaciers have dwindled to 50. According to *Roadside Geology of Montana,* the park should more correctly have been called "Glaciated Park." But do expect awesome views of cirques, tarns, arêtes, horns, hanging valleys, and moraines fashioned thousands of years ago by grinding, groaning conveyor belts of ice.

MINERALS AND METALS

Minerals and metals helped shape the modern cultural history of the Rocky Mountain region. After the fur trade dimmed, people came West looking for gold, silver, copper, lead, and other buried treasures. And they found them. Rocky Mountain rocks are mineral-rich, and the people who first found them got rich too. Minerals and metals now or formerly mined in the region include graphite, gypsum, phosphate, sapphires, travertine, talc, vermiculite, halite, manganese, molybdenum, tungsten, barite, bentonite, fluorspar, chlorite, antimony, chromium, gold, silver, iron, zinc, and lead.

Rocks are basically a conglomeration of different minerals and metal elements. Rocks such as limestone, gneiss, schist, and granite—which abound in the region—often contain valuable minerals.

Some minerals come out of the ground ready to use. Halite (the sodium chloride of table salt) needs little processing before it makes it to the table. There are also placer deposits of metals created when host rock eroded away and the metals were washed down into streambeds. This is why people pan for gold in streams. The promise of gold nuggets from placer deposits drove the Colorado gold rush of the 1880s.

Most of the nuggets have been picked off by now, and today precious metals must be recovered from host rock. This requires a leaching process involving cyanide and other chemicals. In the United States, it usually takes a ton of ore to produce 0.1 troy ounce of gold (1 troy ounce is the equivalent of 1.097 standard ounces). The processing of mined, nonmetallic minerals is less likely to use chemicals. Many minerals can be separated out through magnetism, melting, shaking, crushing, or flotation.

Besides their commercial value, minerals teach us about the region and our planet. Geologists have used minerals to determine the ages of continental basement rock found throughout the Rockies. Minerals in rocks have also helped scientists piece together how dinosaurs died. A thin layer of dark sedimentary rock marks the last days of the Cretaceous period—the end of the age of dinosaurs. Geologists believe the layer was laid down as dust. That dust layer contains mineral grains marked by a pattern of microscopic fractures that happens only when rocks have been violently shattered. The layer also contains an extremely rare variety of quartz called stishovite, which forms only in explosion-shocked rocks. Also found in the dust layer is the element iridium, rare on earth but common to meteorites. The iridium plus fractured minerals provide good evidence that dinosaurs died under a dark dust cloud raised by meteor impact. (See Rocky Mountain Rock)

MOUNTAIN BUILDING

The Rocky Mountains began to rise about 100 million years ago—during the time of the dinosaurs, and about the time flowering plants first arose; long before the first horse, and long, long before the first humans.

At the dawn of the modern Rockies, only a few isolated hills disturbed the flat expanse of western North America. Earlier mountains (including what are known as the "ancestral Rockies") had eroded away, and shallow seas had come and gone. Sediments had filled the basins, leaving what one geology text calls a "monotonous erosion surface."

The stage was set for mountain building about 175 million years ago on the west coast, which was then in Idaho. Due to the subduction of the Pacific Plate under the North American Plate, a volcanic land mass being carried on the Pacific Plate collided with the coast, accreting the land mass onto the continent (if you suddenly feel lost, please see Plate Tectonics). Over millions of years, pressure from that accretion radiated eastward, causing rock in the upper layer of the earth's crust to rumple (fold) like a blanket pushed back on a bed. The rumpling reached the Rocky Mountain region about 100 million years ago, and the mountains began to rise.

By about 45 million years ago, pressure from accretions had stopped and the land began to relax, creating extension faults that caused huge blocks of rock to drop between some ranges.

While the original folding and faulting were going on, another set of forces was at work shaping the Rockies. Between 90 million and 70 million years ago, the subducting Pacific Plate had gotten hot enough to melt continental rocks above it. Enormous volumes of the resultant magma rose like gargantuan bubbles, intruding into upper continental crust in Idaho, western Montana, and British Columbia. Those upwellings of magma cooled underground to

• LEWIS OVERTHRUST •

Most of Glacier National Park is a gigantic slab of rock—2 miles thick in places—that thrust its way northeast at least 35 miles. (Thrust faults occur when layers of rock slip along more or less horizontal planes.) The main overthrust slab became the Lewis Range on the east side of the park. Chief Mountain, in the northeast corner of the park, marks the farthest reach of the slipping slab. Because the fault lies on a horizontal plane, as opposed to being a crack in the ground, the fault line can be traced along the leading edge of the mountains. To the west, the Livingston Range signals a second thrust slab.

Interestingly, the overthrust resulted in very old, Precambrian rocks coming to lie on top of younger, Cretaceous rocks. Both the overthrust slab and the foundation rock are sedimentary. The Precambrian slab contains rocks of the Belt formation which were formed over a billion years ago in an immense lake the stretched from Montana to Canada. (See Bacteria to Apatosaurus) form a group of batholiths—huge masses of granitic rock that may be 100 or more square miles across and 10 to 20 miles thick.

Already rumpled by folding and faulting, the earth's surface was bulged higher by the batholiths. In some cases, bulges got so big that the overlying surface broke into giant slabs. A 10-mile-thick hunk of crust known as the Sapphire block broke off the Idaho batholith and moved about 50 miles east into Montana. The Bitterroot Valley marks the trailing edge of that block.

Still other forces joined in on the mountain construction. About 50 million years ago, widely scattered volcanic eruptions spewed rocks and lava over large parts of the northern Rockies and into south-central Idaho.

After all the folding, relaxing, bulging, and spewing had given the mountains shape, the ranges continued to gain elevation. In fact, most of the gain occurred within the last 5 million years, possibly as a result of the earth's crust floating up to find some geologic equilibrium (isostatic adjustment). Rivers and streams in existence before this recent uplift cut downward as fast as the land rose, creating such deep river canyons as Royal Gorge, near Canon City, Colorado. The Colorado River was another erosion machine; geologists think that much of the Grand Canyon

Subduction and Mountain Building

was carved in just the last
2 million to 3 million years.

And it ain't over till it's over.
The Rockies continue to rise,
as evidenced by occasional
measurable growth spurts
gained during earthquakes. (See
Earthquakes; Plate Tectonics)

PLATE TECTONICS

As you enjoy the sweeping
views from some high,
scenic vista, thank plate tectonics.

To understand how the Rocky
Mountains came into being, one
must first understand the
relatively simple dynamics of
plate tectonics. To understand
tectonics, one must first
remember that the earth has
3 layers—core, mantle, and crust.
Plate tectonics is a manifestation
of the interactions between the
mantle and crust.

The mantle, made of a black
rock called peridotite, is mostly
solid, but is so super-hot that it
flows in sluggish convection
currents. The crust is broken into

about 8 major plates, which float
around on mantle convection
currents, moving at a rate of about
1 to 2 inches per year. The 2 plates
relevant to the Rocky Mountains
are the North American Plate and
the Pacific Plate.

Technically speaking, each
tectonic plate is composed of a
slab of crust fused to a rigid skim
layer of upper mantle. The crust
plus this skim backing is called
the lithosphere.

Plates can carry continents,
oceans, or both. Some plates meet
under an ocean; some meet where
the sea borders a continent. Some
plates are traveling away from
each other, others are colliding,
and still others just slide past
each other.

In the Rockies, we are most
interested in colliding plates.
Continental crust is lighter
than oceanic crust, so when the
Pacific Plate crashed into the
North American Plate, the North
American Plate began to ride
over the Pacific Plate, pushing it

down. This process is called subduction—and it's still happening, right this very second.

Another collision-related tectonic process relevant to mountain building is called accretion. Actually, accretion is a byproduct of subduction. Imagine a fictional island in the Pacific Ocean. As North America rides over the subducting Pacific Plate, that island eventually meets the shore. In the end, the island gets scraped off the diving plate and "accreted" onto the edge of the continent.

North America's west coast used to be in Idaho. Washington, Oregon, and most of Alaska are composed of accreted land.

It's hard to overestimate the influence plate tectonics has had on earth history. Plate tectonics causes earthquakes, builds mountains, produces volcanoes, and even creates new landforms—all of which affect our geography and climate, which affect the existence and evolution of life forms.

RIVERS

A number of major rivers originate in the northern and central Rocky Mountains. Their waters disperse across the country according to their place along the Continental Divide—eventually flowing into the Pacific Ocean, Gulf of Mexico, or Gulf of California.

Born in Teton County, Wyoming, the Snake River runs for 40 miles through Grand Teton National Park. An accurate, and perhaps lovelier, name for Jackson Hole could have been Snake River Valley. Once out of the park, the 1,038-mile-long river flows into Idaho, crossing that state and then turning north up the Idaho border, through Hells Canyon. At Lewiston, Idaho, the river bends west into Washington, where it

> **North America's west coast used to be in Idaho.**

joins the Columbia River. The Columbia carries Snake water the rest of the way out to the Pacific Ocean. Major tributaries to the Snake include the Salmon and Clearwater Rivers.

The headwaters of the Yellowstone River are high in the wilderness area just south of Yellowstone National Park. However, most people first see the river in the park as it scrambles out of Yellowstone Lake, one of the largest high-elevation lakes in North America, with a shoreline of over 100 miles. After leaving the lake, the river flows through the Hayden Valley before plunging over 2 waterfalls: the 109-foot Upper Falls and the 308-foot Lower Falls, which is twice as high as Niagara Falls. At the bottom of the falls, the river travels through a steep, 20-mile-long canyon.

The Yellowstone flows out of the park at the north entrance in Gardiner, Montana. From there it flows northeast across the state

Rocky Mountain Rivers

and joins the Missouri River inside the North Dakota border at the Fort Union National Historic Site. The Missouri transports Yellowstone water the rest of the way to the Gulf of Mexico. Although the 692-mile-long Yellowstone isn't totally free of human manipulation, it remains

• JOHN WESLEY POWELL •

After the Civil War, the U.S. government authorized geological and geographical exploration of the western territories. The ambitious expeditions resulted in a string of important discoveries, including rich mineral deposits and fossil beds that yielded previously undescribed plants and animals. The dramatic and exposed western geology—the likes of which had never been seen by easterners—also led to new theories of how landscapes evolve.

One of the most remarkable characters to emerge during that period of discovery was Major John Wesley Powell. The one-armed Powell led the first documented expedition down the Colorado River in 1869, departing from Green River, Wyoming, on May 24, with 10 men in 4 wooden boats. Three months later, Powell and his men arrived—in 3 boats—in southern Nevada where the Virgin River joins the Colorado near what is now Las Vegas. A second, more exhaustively planned expedition was launched in 1871 to survey and chart the region. Powell's survey filled in the last, large blank on the North American map—a region that included large parts of what are now Utah and Arizona.

In 1879, after much lobbying, Powell's survey was joined with 3 other official western surveys to create the original U.S. Geological Survey. The major was appointed the second director of the USGS, serving that agency for 14 years.

An enthusiastic student of Native American cultures, Powell also founded the U.S. Bureau of Ethnology in 1879 and directed it until his death in 1902.

one of the longest undammed rivers in the West.

The Missouri River itself isn't born up in the high country, but begins by declaration in a broad, southwestern Montana valley where 3 mountain rivers come together. The Gallatin, Madison, and Jefferson Rivers meet near Three Forks, Montana, to form the headwaters of the Missouri. The river flows generally north from Three Forks to Great Falls, Montana, where it once cascaded dramatically over a series of waterfalls. The falls were flooded in modern times by dams constructed to provide hydroelectricity.

Of course, there were no dams when Lewis and Clark traveled the Missouri by cottonwood canoe, and the falls presented the Corps of Discovery with the most formidable portage of the entire journey. It took the men nearly a month to detour 18 miles around the falls.

From Great Falls, the 3,710-mile-long Missouri turns eastward into North Dakota and then bends south through South Dakota into Nebraska, where it forms the border with Iowa, and finally into Missouri, where it joins the Mississippi at St. Louis, running eventually into the Gulf of Mexico.

The headwaters of the Colorado River are in the high, formerly glaciated Kawuneeche Valley of Rocky Mountain National Park. At its very beginning, the mighty Colorado is more like a creek, nearly small enough to jump over. Beavers are

said to dam it regularly, starting a trend that continues downriver.

A bit of boosterism put the Colorado headwaters in Rocky Mountain National Park. Two tributaries actually come together to form the Colorado: the Green River and the Grand River. But in 1921, Colorado legislators convinced Congress to officially extend the Colorado north, essentially substituting the Colorado's name for the Grand, making the park the official birthplace of one of North America's greatest rivers.

From Kawuneeche Valley, the 1,450-mile-long Colorado flows through Colorado into Utah, where it backs up from Glen Canyon Dam, just over the border in Arizona, and continues through Arizona and the Grand Canyon. From there, the river traces part of the Arizona–Nevada border disguised as the Lake Mead Reservoir, then continues along the Arizona–California border before passing through Mexico to the Gulf of California.

Eleven federal hydropower plants on the Colorado generate enough electrical power to serve 3 million people, with enough surplus to meet the partial energy requirements of 9 million to 12 million more consumers. Colorado River water is also diverted to irrigate 3.5 million acres of cropland in 6 states.

ROCKY MOUNTAIN ROCK

The forces of plate tectonics have kept the region's rocks shifting, folding, thrusting, spewing, bulging, and buckling. After tectonics did the heavy lifting, wind and water have worked to further expose the Rockies' stony face.

Some people read historical novels; other people read rocks. Once you know the geological vocabulary, rocks can be as full of intrigue, suspense, and surprise endings as any bestseller.

All rocks fall into 1 of 3 classes depending on how they were formed: sedimentary, igneous, or metamorphic.

Sedimentary rock typically begins as mud, sand, silt, or the shells of small aquatic animals accumulated on the bottom of a lake, river, or ocean. As additional sediment layers accumulate over time, lower layers turn to rock. Fossil hunters key in on sedimentary rocks because if an animal or plant is covered by sediments before decay sets in, a fossil may result. Sandstone, shale, mudstone, limestone, and dolomite are all sedimentary. Limestone may be "fossiliferous," containing patterns of visible fossils.

Sedimentary rocks are also created through a process in which minerals precipitate out of water—such as what happens when stalagmites form in caves or travertine precipitates out of hot springs.

Because the Rocky Mountain region used to be covered by Precambrian lakes, then later by a sea, sedimentary rocks are abundant. Many of those rocks were uplifted by mountain-building events, so look for huge limestone reefs exposed in mountainsides, and keep an eye out for marine fossils on summits composed of sedimentary rock.

Igneous rocks are formed by magma (molten rock). There are 2 types: intrusive and extrusive. Intrusive igneous rocks cool while still underground—the granite of a batholith, for example. Uplift and erosion have exposed batholiths and granitic basement rock around the Rockies; you'll find a spectacular view of the Boulder Batholith east of Butte on Homestake Pass.

Extrusive rocks cool above the surface, such as the basalt rock formed from flowing lava, or pumice formed from white-hot flying ash. Intermittent periods of intense volcanic activity have spread igneous rock and ash layers throughout the region. In many cases, volcanic layers cover older sedimentary rock. Near Yellowstone, in parts of the Absaroka Range, volcanic rocks surround logs petrified by the hot ash flows that smothered them. Layers of petrified forests developed in this area of the Rockies when soil formed on weathered ash and lava, trees grew, and then another volcanic event buried the forest. More soil would eventually form on the new layer of ash and lava, trees would grow, and the cycle would be repeated.

Metamorphic rock is formed when layers of sedimentary and igneous rock are subjected to extreme heat and pressure by tectonic forces. These rocks typically appear banded because the metamorphic squeeze causes minerals within the rock to reassemble into layers. Limestone and dolomite metamorphose into

> **Rocks can be as full of intrigue, suspense, and surprise endings as any bestseller.**
>
> ●

marble, while shale and mudstone turn to schist or, under greater pressure, to slate. Granite or sandstone can be metamorphosed into gneiss.

Gneiss and schist are exposed in places throughout the Rockies. In the Front Range of Colorado, gneiss and schist erode to jagged crags, while granites of the Front erode to rounder knobs and domes. Remember what geologists say: don't take a gneiss rock for granite.

There is definitely geological reincarnation. Sedimentary rocks become metamorphic rocks, which become exposed and are eroded into the sand and silt of future sedimentary rock. Metamorphic rock may become so hot underground that it melts, setting the stage for the formation of igneous rocks, which erode into sediments, and on and on.

ROCKY MOUNTAIN TRENCH

The Rocky Mountain trench is most familiar to geologists, who know it as an ancient glacial valley, and to pilots, who use the trench as a 900-mile-long landmark to navigate northwest into the Yukon Territory as the crow flies. Plain old citizens know their own piece of the trench by other names, including the Mission, Flathead, and Tobacco Valleys. Or, U.S. Highway 93, north from St. Ignatius, Montana.

The trench runs from St. Ignatius all the way through the Canadian province of British Columbia into the Yukon. And it is a trench—a trough between 2 mountain ranges for much of its length. The trench was formed during the ice ages by a glacier that managed to push as far south as the Mission and southern Swan Valleys of northwestern Montana. The weight of the ice depressed underlying sediments, helping form the trough. Near the Canadian border, ice was deep enough to nearly cover the mountains, but the glacier thinned to the south, forming a long tongue of ice.

Stromatolites flourished in a vast, shallow body of water called the Belt Lake that stretched from south-central Montana northwest through Idaho and Washington into British Columbia. The lake formed about 1.4 billion years ago and existed quietly for about 200 million years, laying down sediments that would harden into what we now call Belt rocks—extensive formations of red, green, purple, and gray sandstone, mudstone, and limestone prominent in Glacier National Park and found throughout the northern Rockies. Belt rocks are named for the Belt Mountains of Montana, where they were first studied.

When the Belt rocks were forming, bacteria and algae were the only life forms on the face of the earth, and our modern, oxygen-containing atmosphere was just developing. Although dinosaurs are the charismatic macrofossils of the West, trace fossils left in the Belt rocks are perhaps even more awesome, if simply for the time period they represent. The flooding and receding water left its mark in delicate ripple patterns, mud cracks, and even dimples made by rain pattering on soft mud. Look for these stunning mementos of our developing planet in almost any outcrop of Belt rocks.

Various bodies of water followed the Belt Lake to inundate the land that is now the Rocky Mountain region. About 370 million years ago, the still-flat area was covered with a warm sea teeming with a variety of marine species, including corals, spongelike animals, squid ancestors, and armored fishes. Today, it is possible to find marine fossils high in some Rocky Mountain ranges, lifted there as the mountains rose up after the sea had long gone.

About 75 million years ago, another interior sea flooded North America from the rising Rockies east through the Great Basin. Dinosaurs walked on the western shores of that sea, and a rare few were preserved as tantalizing clues for us to find and ponder.

Stromatolites

Geologists have determined that the trench runs parallel to the eastern front of a thrust fault that extends from the Canadian Rockies into Montana.

In the trench, look for anomalous streamlined hills, especially near Eureka, Montana. These hills, called drumlins, are formed somewhat near the terminus, or foot, of the glacier as rocky debris is moved along at the bottom. Exactly how drumlins form is the subject of some controversy, but everyone pretty much agrees on their identity. The authors of *Roadside Geology of Montana* write that an aerial view of drumlins suggests "schools of giant tadpoles all lined up with their big heads facing upstream, their slender tails pointing downstream."

STROMATOLITE

Although the Rocky Mountains themselves are fairly young, their uplifted rocks contain trace fossils of the most ancient life forms.

The earth was formed about 4.6 billion years ago and was apparently lifeless for the first 1.5 billion years. Around that time, a mysterious chain of events caused chemical elements present on the planet to combine in a way that gave rise to living bacteria.

About 3 billion years ago, pioneering cyanobacteria began to form colonies of matlike mounds in the warm, shallow waters of an oxygenless earth, similar to the mats of algae and bacteria still present in thermal features of Yellowstone National Park. Like green plants, the bacteria produced food through photosynthesis, using energy from the sun and carbon dioxide from the water.

The bacteria secreted slime to provide protection from ultraviolet radiation and other environmental hazards, but the slime also collected silt. When the silt layer got so thick that sunlight couldn't get through, the colony would ooze up through the muck and establish a new microbial layer. This sliming and silting eventually produced layered formations called stromatolites ("stone mattresses"). In the absence of any competing organisms, stromatolites ruled the world for the next 2 billion years—which is a good thing, since their exhalations of oxygen eventually built the atmosphere we breathe today.

Scientists can speak with some authority about the biology of stromatolites, since living equivalents were found in the 1950s in Australia and Florida.

Hunt for fossil stromatolites in Glacier National Park in road cuts west of Logan Pass and along the trail from Logan Pass to Hidden Lake. They look like the scrolled clouds of Vincent van Gogh paintings, or like cabbage heads in section view. You can also see 2-billion-year-old fossil stromatolites west of Laramie, Wyoming, where the Snowy Range Highway crosses the Medicine Bow Mountains.

YELLOWSTONE CALDERA AND HOT SPOT

About 600,000 years ago, in what is now Yellowstone Park, a couple of giant pools of magma pushed up through the earth's crust to within a few

thousand feet of the surface. Heat and pressure from the upwelling magma caused the ground to bulge and split, and small rivers of lava began to flow. Eventually, a series of explosions sent white-hot rock, ash, and pumice hurling across the landscape. This searing debris blanketed the region, filling in valleys and depositing extensive sheets of material that cooled into a rock type called ash-flow tuff.

Hundreds of cubic miles of earth and rock were displaced during the explosions, and when the dust settled, what ground was left collapsed into the now-empty magma chambers. At that point, the Yellowstone Caldera, or crater, was probably over half a mile deep and as many as 45 miles across. It's still possible to detect the caldera, although subsequent lava flows have partially filled it back in.

How and why did such a volume of molten rock rise so close to the surface in that one place? Some researchers think the answer lies in a phenomenon they call the Yellowstone Hot Spot.

Lava flowed into the Yellowstone Caldera at temperatures above 1,500°F. To be heated to such extremes, the magma had to come from deep inside the earth. Scientists think that a plume of super-hot magma rose through the earth's mantle, somewhat like a geyser, from near the earth's core. They surmise that the plume pooled near the surface before it erupted, creating a "hot spot."

Since the North American Plate is moving southwest, the hot spot would show up in different surface locations over time. Imagine passing your hand above a candle flame. Your hand, the crust, moves while the hot spot stays put. Actually, the hot spot does get dragged a bit by the lithosphere and seems to move with the plate at a rate of about 15 miles per million years.

Some 40 hot spots have been identified around the globe, nearly all located under oceans, with a spot under Hawaii. If a true hot spot does lie beneath Yellowstone, its position below a continent would be unique.

The Yellowstone explosion was just the most recent eruption of the hot spot. The Picabo volcanic field (northwest of Pocatello, Idaho), the Heise volcanic field (north of Idaho Falls), and the Yellowstone volcanic field are lined up in a way that matches the movement of the plate, and those 3 are progressively younger volcanic centers. If the trend continues, calculations indicate that the next eruption may be between Cooke City and Red Lodge, Montana—and on to North Dakota.

Since eruptions seem to occur every 600,000 to 800,000 years, we may have to wait only 100,000 years or so to find out what happens next.

FURTHER READING

Craighead, John J., Frank C. Craighead, and Ray J. Davis. *A Field Guide to Rocky Mountain Wildflowers*. Boston: Houghton Mifflin Company, 1963.

Ehrlich, Paul R., David S. Dobkin, and Darryl Wheye. *The Birder's Handbook: A Field Guide to the Natural History of North American Birds*. New York: Simon and Schuster/Fireside Books, 1988.

Fitzgerald, James P., Carron A. Meany, and David Armstrong. *Mammals of Colorado*. Niwot, Colorado: University Press of Colorado and Denver Museum of Natural History, 1994.

Gould, Stephen J., gen. ed. *The Book of Life: An Illustrated History of the Evolution of Life on Earth*. New York: W.W. Norton & Company, 1993.

Hart, Jeff. *Montana Native Plants and Early Peoples*. Helena, Montana: Montana Historical Society Press, 1976.

Koch, Edward D., and Charles R. Peterson. *Amphibians and Reptiles of Yellowstone and Grand Teton National Parks*. Salt Lake City: University of Utah Press, 1995.

Nelson, Ruth Ashton, rev. by Roger L. Williams. *Handbook of Rocky Mountain Plants*. Niwot, Colorado: Robert Rinehart Publishers and Denver Museum of Natural History, 1992.

Riebsame, William E., gen. ed. *Atlas of the New West: Portrait of a Changing Region*. New York: W.W. Norton & Company, 1997. A project of the Center of the American West, University of Colorado, Boulder.

Roadside Geology of. . . . series. Missoula: Mountain Press Publishing Company. Volumes available for Idaho, Montana, Yellowstone Country, Wyoming, Colorado.

Ulrich, Tom J. *Birds of the Northern Rockies*. Missoula: Mountain Press Publishing Company, 1984.

Wassink, Jan L. *Mammals of the Central Rockies*. Missoula: Mountain Press Publishing Company, 1993.

ABOUT THE AUTHOR

Susan Ewing is the author of three other books: *The Great Alaska Nature Factbook*; the wildlife travelogue *Going Wild in Washington and Oregon*; and *Lucky Hares and Itchy Bears*, a book of children's animal verse. Her work has also appeared in various anthologies including *Solo: On Her Own Adventure*, *Alaska Passages*, and *American Nature Writing 1997*, and in such magazines as *Sports Afield*, *Gray's Sporting Journal*, and *Fly Rod & Reel*.

She moved to the northern Rockies in 1992 from Alaska and the Pacific Northwest, and lives in Montana with a fisherman, three dogs, and two falcons.

INDEX